NOT JUST ANOTHER COMPUTER BOOK - REVISED

by

Dr. Alfonso J. Kinglow

Copyright © 2021 Alfonso J. Kinglow
All rights reserved.
ISBN: 9-781304-488800

Printed in The United States of America

DEDICATION

I would like to Dedicate this book to my wife Sarah for her continued support and dedication to my Projects to bring New Computer Technology to Seniors and Beginners and to my children and grand children; you made me a Proud father, Grand Father and a better man.

My Children, and Grand Children;

My **Strength**

My **Light** and

My **Joy**

My Daughters

Kezia, Keren and Karina

Who inspired me to leave some of my vast knowledge behind for posterity, and For my First Grand-son **Kenny,** "Te-Sho" Virtue and Longevity and my

First Grand-daughter " **Aia**" Anaiah, Patience, Purity and Power

I Love you all. " Wo oi di "   " Di Hau-Li-An "

CONTENTS

CHAPTERS

1	The ALU – Arithmetic Logic Unit	1
2	Minimum Hardware Requirements	Pg #
3	The Bit and CPU Speed	Pg #
4	Computer Hardware Ports-Desktop	Pg #
5	Viruses	Pg #
6	Computer Networks Adapters	Pg #
7	The Internet World Wide Web	Pg #
8	Application Software Tools	Pg #
9	The All Applications folder	Pg #
10	Basic Computer Terms	Pg #

| 11 | Application Software | Pg # |
| 10 | Fixed and Wireless Printers | Pg # |

PREFACE

After reviewing many computer books over the years, I discovered that they all assume that the reader's have some basic knowledge of computers and that they understand the entire computer lingo's that are used. All of their assumptions are wrong, and lead sometimes to misconceptions.

Almost all of the computer books I reviewed did not have, or did not include basic computer terms used, or did not explain the meaning of some basic computer concepts., or the use of Windows Tools, some hidden and some built-in where the users could have access. I started to include all of these concepts and tools in my new books. When this book was first published in 2014 we did not have the Windows Technologies that we have now. In this Revision of 2021 I am including some of these Tools and Concepts.

This Revised Book is a recommended starting place for anyone wanting to know the Basics of Computers and of Windows OS System Setup and configurations.

This book assumes nothing, and present Basic Computer information in a plain and simple format, which includes some hidden features and commands that all users should know; but are not published.

These hidden features are Basic information and Tools built into the hardware and software, but were not considered important enough by Microsoft for the Users to know, and were kept hidden.

This book is Revised to give the user a complete knowledge of Computer Hardware and Software and current related Standard's up to date., the original version was published in 2014 and since then new Standards and New Technologies have been released and updated., as new Technologies and the New **Windows 11** is about to be Release this year in 2021 which will bring new and exciting Technologies for all Users and all levels.

An emphasis is placed on current and new Standards that have been Updated and Released this year., and why they are important. We review the current Wireless Standard (802.11 b/g/**x**) and the Standards **AC, AD** and **AX**.

We also explain the "defacto" Standards that are used in Computer Technologies.

This basic knowledge help's the reader to understand why some hardware and software features that are used, operate the way they do, and explains the differences between Standards related to Computer Networks, Hardware and Software.

The material presented provides an in-depth of introductory computer subjects; which includes how to use computers, how to access information and data on computer networks and the Internet World Wide Web, and hidden features and commands embedded into your computer hardware and software and revealed in this Revised version.

This new Revision will:

- Present the most up to date Computer Technology
- Teach the basic concepts of hardware and software
- Present the material in a way that seniors and students can understand it, using simple comprehensive methods and charts.
- Present a basic understanding of Local Area Networks (LAN) and Wide Area Networks (WAN) and Wireless Networks.
- Present basic information on how to secure your computer
- Present the most up to date technology on computer security hardware and software.
- Give students an in-depth understanding of why computers are used in business, academia, government, industry and society today.
- Present strategies that seniors and students can use to install secure and maintain their desktop and laptop computers.
- Present some of the hidden software and utilities in Windows 8
- Show the users how to use SNAPIN's and the Microsoft Management Console (MMC).
- Present information on Free and Paid Antivirus Programs
- Present information on how to use Email and Email Applications.
- Present complete and comprehensive information on the Internet and the World Wide Web.
- Present information on setting up Wireless Networks and using WI-FI on the Internet.

- Complete information on using the Internet Search Engines and Search operators.
- Present information on Free Software available for Download
- Present information on Freeware, Shareware, Trialware and Public Domain Software.
- Present information on Cleaning and Protecting Computers
- General Information on The first Rule of Protection for Computers, and **The Rule of 30.**
- Present information about user Applications and System Applications.
- General information on the different Search Engines on the Internet.

CHAPTER 1
UNO

ALU   Arithmetic Logic Unit

Any computer consist of three major parts, the input, the output and the
ALU. The input is the keyboard, the mouse, a flash drive, the Ethernet or Internet connection, a microphone, a camera, etc.. Anything that enters data into the computer using one of the many computer ports. The output is the video display, or video monitor, the printer, a video recorder, etc.. The ALU is the arithmetic logic unit which contains the CPU, central processing unit, the memory, or random access memory called RAM, the storage hard drive or HD and the OS or operating system.

The operating system or OS is part of the Software, and the rest of the components are part of the Hardware. Your computer operation will require using both the hardware and the software together.

They are minimum Hardware requirements in order to efficiently use the Software OS. The minimum requirements also will affect the User Software programs that will be installed on the computer.

Most computers will already have the Software OS such as Windows 7 or 8 already installed with some User Software. Most of the User Software will be Trialware, there will be some free Games and Utilities installed.

Trialware software will only have limited capabilities and will only work for a period of 30 to 60 days sometimes, some Trialware software do not install the complete version of the software and only a basic portion is
installed, after the trial time; the user will be required to
purchase a license to install the full version of the software. The Trialware version will then have to be un-installed correctly in order to remove it safely from your computer before you can install the full license version of the software.

It is recommended that you install a full version of the software you want to use and not install Trialware software on your computer. Your computer may also come with a Trialware version of some kind of Antivirus software.

It is very important to note that the Trialware version of the Antivirus program will not fully protect your computer. After a short period of time you will also be required to purchase a full version of the Antivirus program.

You may install in the mean time a Free version of any Antivirus program; such as (.AVG) which is a Freeware Application. This will provide some Basic protection to your system, until you can install a complete Antivirus program.

The Free AVG Antivirus is a complete antivirus application, with the basic necessary modules to protect your computer. You may purchase the full application at any time which will give you more capabilities and protection. It is better to install Freeware Applications than any Trialware Application. You may also find many Public Domain Software that are very useful and are also free.

If you are looking for applications and utilities for your computer, you may find useful software in Public Domain, Open Source, and Freeware Software on the Internet. All these categories contain software that are free to use and download, and are not " Trialware".

Setup and Turn on your Computer for the first time.
—

To turn on the Computer, press the Power Button, the button with the circle. When the computer starts up

Windows will start to load. If your Operating System (OS) is Windows 8 or higher, you will see a series of "Tiles" representing several parts of the computer and software that is installed. The most important Tile is the tile called " Desktop", from this tile you will setup the computer.

Desktop is located on the left side of the screen, aprox. The second tile up from the bottom. it will be labeled Desktop., click on it to display the Desktop. The Desktop will have a background screen; if it does not, then you need to setup and personalize the desktop.

To setup the desktop background screen, click anywhere on the desktop and select " Personalize" from the Menu.

Select a Theme, from Windows, Earth or Flowers then click on "Desktop Background" to exit.

Your desktop should only have the icons that are necessary to navigate Windows. Most new computers will have installed a lot of different applications that are " Trialware" and junk.

The most important Icons that should be displayed on your Desktop are: Computer, or My Computer or My PC, next is Network, then Recycle Bin or the Trash Can. And IE Internet Explorer, the Microsoft built in Web Browser to navigate the Internet, and an Antivirus program to protect your computer. These five(5) Applications is what the Desktop should have.

Windows 7 and Windows 8 will have a Start Button on the lower left side of the screen, followed by a big blue E that represents IE or Internet Explorer, followed by a Folder which contains the Libraries.

Once your Desktop is setup, proceed to setting up your computer or PC. Move the cursor to lower corner on the right side of the screen to display the Windows "CHARMS".

The Windows Charms will display five (5) Symbols, select the first Symbol that looks like a Spoke Wheel, which is " Settings." When the Settings window is displayed, it will be a blue window, go to the bottom of the window and select" Change PC Settings" to begin the SETUP of your Computer.

There will be thirteen (13) sections approximately to setup. Go down each section and follow the instructions on the screen for that section to set that section up then move to the other sections, one at a time. At the end of the thirteenth section, put your cursor back to the bottom to display the CHARMS again and go to the START Symbol, which will be in the middle, and select it to go back to the Desktop.

When you are back on the Desktop, go to the Start Button on the left side of the screen and "Restart" the computer.

When the computer starts up again, it will be Configured with the Options you selected during the Setup process.

Your Computer is now Ready for operations.

Microsoft **EDGE** replaced IE Internet Explorer, or you can use any other Web Browser like **FIREFOX**, or **BING,** they are free, download them from www.firefox.com or www.bing.com

Launch Bing or Firefox or Edge first by double-clicking on its Icon, to get on the Internet and also to check your Network to see if you are connected to the Internet.

To Shutdown the Computer Safely._____

To shutdown the Computer safely: Hold down or Press the "**ALT**" key on the keyboard and press the Function Key **F4** at the same time. The **ALT Key** is located on the left side of the keyboard next to the Windows key, (The key with the Flag on it); the F4 key is the fourth key from the first row of keys on the keyboard. You can also access **Task-Manager** and Shutdown from Task Manager, on the Power Circle on the right side lower part of the screen. To access the Task-Manager hold down the **CTRL+ALT+DEL** Keys at the same time., from your Keyboard.

Another method is to use the **Start button,** on the lower left side of the screen and click on it to display the shutdown tab, then select " shutdown" to shutdown the computer.

Utilities included in Windows Operating Systems. ____

Windows 7 and 8 as well as **Windows 10** include several utility programs. A File Manager, that does all functions related to File Management. An Image Viewer, that displays and copies the contents of graphics files. An Uninstaller, that removes a program and any entries associated in the system. A Disk scanner that detects and corrects problems on a disk, a disk Defragmenter, that reorganizes the files and unused space on the computer hard disk, a Diagnostic Utility, that reports technical information about the computer's hardware and software programs. To run the Diagnostic utility, type in the search or start box, **DXDiag** to call up the utility. A Backup Utility, that is used to copy and back up selected files and or the entire Hard Disk (C: >Drive). A Screen Saver that displays a moving image or blank screen. If no keyboard or mouse activity is detected.

Stand-Alone Utility Programs. ____

Stand-Alone Utility programs offer improvements over features built into the Operating System or provides features not included in the Operating System. An Antivirus Program , protects computers against Viruses,

Worms and Trojans. <u>The Antivirus program must be installed on the Computer.</u> Some Antivirus programs are Free and are available on the Internet to Download. The best **FREE Antivirus** program is **AVG**. Download AVG from www.avg.com from the Company **Iobit.** Its Free.

A Personal Firewall, detects and protects computers from unauthorized intrusions. A File Compression Utility, shrinks the size of a file so that it takes up less storage space. In **Windows 7 and 8, or Windows 10;** the File Compression utility appears as a Folder with a Zipper across it. To display this folder, right click on any blank spot on the desktop to display the Menu that contains the folder. Also called a "Zip Folder".

A personal Computer Maintenance Utility, identifies and repairs operating system problems or disk problems, and improves a Computer Performance.

CHAPTER 2
DOS

Minimum Hardware Requirements for your Computer.__ Updated to 2021.

Your computer hardware must have the following minimum requirements in order to run more efficiently software applications and the (OS) Operating System, such as **Windows 8.0, 8.1 or Windows 10.** The best Windows Operating System for any Computer today is **Windows 10 Pro.** The Professional version.

Windows 10 now have many versions: Do not buy Computers with Windows 10 HOME, or Windows 10 Basic, or Windows 10 Standard, or Windows 10 Student Editions. To be able to **UPGRADE** to **WINDOWS 11** you must have **Windows 10 Pro.**

1. Processor INTEL or AMD 2.1 Ghz to 2.8 Ghz or higher, If Processor speeds are below 2.0 Ghz it will be very Slow.
2. Processor speeds above 2.0 Ghz will be faster and very fast, if the Processor is a Dual-Core i-3, i-5, i-7, i-9 or higher, made by Intel; they will be extremely fast.
3. Recommended Processors: **i-7 or i-9 made by INTEL.**

4. Ram-Memory 2, 4, 8, or 16 Gigabytes is recommended, ODD Memory is **unacceptable such as 3Gb or 6Gb or 12** Gb. As the Memory does not conform to the International Standards and Computers will not work correctly.

> Computers with this type of memory is usually sharing the
> Memory with the Computer Desktop Screen and Video. Ram Memory must always be EVEN   (1-2-4-8-16-32-64GB) etc..

5. Hard Drive Storage should be **1 Tb to 2 Tb** (Terabytes) internal, however; you may also have an External USB drive of 1 Tb or higher, for Backup or to extend the storage capacity of your computer.

> **The Computer Battery.__**
>
> The Computer Battery will be a **Lithium-Ion Battery,** which is most common among Laptops, and is not very expensive. The best batteries are **CERAMIC** and **MAGNESIUM** Batteries; and are very expensive. The Lithium – Ion battery shelf life is usually around 2 years or less, with a use of 2 to 4 hours a Day. This Battery tends to get hot and may require a Fan underneath the Laptop, to keep the hardware cool.
>
> The other type of Battery is a **Polymer battery,** which cost a little more but has a better shelf-life and

longer use time. This Battery also will last longer and will not get hot. This Battery is recommended.

The other Battery is a **Magnesium Battery,** this battery will be more expensive and last a long time. May have a shelf-life of 5 to 7 years or more, and a use of 12 hours or more. This is the best battery, but its heavier, as compared to Lithium-Ion which is much lighter.

Windows OS Versions. ___

The recommended Software OS should be the Professional version of the software. **Windows 10Pro is recommended.** Windows 8 Professional is far better than Windows 8 Home, Student or Basic editions. Windows 8 operates in 32 bit mode or 64 bit mode. **Sixty four (64 Bit) mode is faster and is recommended** if you are going to use more than 4 Gb of Ram Memory. Windows 8 in 32 bit mode works just fine if you have 4 Gb of Ram Memory or higher.

New users to Windows 8 will notice that the OS does not have a START button. If you would like to have a Start button, because you are familiar with this capability from previous versions, you may install one.

    10. **The Windows 8 Start button** is a free application that is available on the Internet, other free applications are also available for download at several Web sites. You may do a Search on

Freeware Software and Public Domain Software to get these applications and or utilities.

It is recommended that you upgrade your computer to Windows 10. The new Windows 8.1 Upgrade removed the Start button and other basic components from the Desktop. It is recommended that you stay with Windows 8 until the new **Windows 10 or 11** is released. Since very soon **Windows 11** will be coming out, it will require some review. The Windows Operating System is evolving very quickly to provide the users with better and faster technologies.

Please note that we the Users are the one's that are driving the technology, we are demanding better and faster hardware and software. We want more and faster applications and multimedia software. Large Software companies such as Microsoft Corporation, and other's; are trying to keep up with the user's demands.

We are now using more social media applications to communicate via the internet, such as Facebook and Twitter, and these companies are also trying to keep up with the user's demands.

Computers are now a necessity and are required in every household in America and elsewhere, as a very essential tool for business and or entertainment.

The speed of your computer will depend on the type of Processor in your computer, with the amount of Ram Memory installed.

INTEL is the largest manufacturer of Computer Chips and Computer Processors in the World, followed by AMD and others.

Intel Dual-Core Processors i-5, to i-7 and i-9 are very fast processors and are now available in some laptops and desktops computers. It is recommended that you get a computer with one of these processors, with a storage capacity of at least **1 Tb** minimum, up to **2 Tb**. Internal hard drive.

Faster Processors are been developed, which will change the way we do business and Technology in general. The important thing to remember is that the CPU or Central Processing Unit determines the Speed of your computer with the installed RAM -Random Access Memory. Minimum RAM should be 8 Gb or higher.

CPU should have a minimum speed of 2.5 to 2.8 Giga- hertz or GHz.

CHAPTER 3
TRES

The Bit and your Computer Processor Speed.__

The smallest unit of information that can be transmitted over the internet or to and from your computer is called a Bit.

The Bit is a binary number that represents 0 (zero) or 1 (one).

Using just these two numerical characters you can transmit any message you want to a computer since every letter in the alphabet has a binary equivalent sets of numbers, representing 8 bits.; such as 01100111. Since bits are very small they had to be divided and organized to handle large amounts of **Data** to facilitate **Storage** and distribution.

So, 8 Bits is equal to *1 Byte* and 8 Bytes is equal to *1 Word* .

The following terms are therefore used in all Computers to designate thousands and millions of Bytes: *Kilo-bytes* is equal to one thousand bytes, *Mega-Bytes* is equal to 1 Million bytes, *Giga-bytes* is equal to 1 Trillion Bytes, *Tera-bytes* is equal to 1 Billion Bytes, etc.. These values are used in computers for storage and to designate computer memory.

In the case of designating Processor speeds, a different term is used to represent cycles per second or (cps) which is also designated in hertz, used in the name of the German Physicist that discovered it. So we say that processor speeds are measured in cycles per second or (cps) or we can also say in hertz or (hz).

The speed of processors are always in Giga-hertz or Giga-cycles per second (Ghz). A fast processor should be above 2.0 Ghz per second. Anything below 2.0Ghz will be very slow. A processor speed above 2.0Ghz will be very fast. Fast computers have processors that are 2.5 Ghz to 3.0Ghz or higher., To achieve very fast speeds, processors are built with Dual-Core, which will have more that one processors. Some computer manufacturers chips will contain dual core processors running seven (7) or more processors and are designated with the "I" Code, such as Intel Processor Dual-Core i-7. To get a fast computer, make sure you meet the above requirements of a fast Processor and a very large storage for your data. Most computers will have at least a storage hard drive of at least 500 Gb (Giga-bytes) of storage or higher. You can now buy external hard drives for storage in the tera-byte range. In designating computer memory, a division was selected to facilitate operation and distribution of in line memory modules that were single or dual so thay could be used in various types of computers. These memory modules were called (SIMM's) or single in-line memory modules, and (DIMM's) Dual in-line memory modules, and Random access memory or (RAM). Memory used in computers were divided as 1, 2, 4, 8, 16, 32, 64 Gb (Giga bytes) of Ram memory or higher, always EVEN MULTIPLE numbers to meet computer standards. Computers with ODD MULTIPLE numbers are not acceptable, because the computer memory is shared with other parts of the computer such as the Video Display, not leaving enough memory for the system and or applications, and may not fully meet US or International Standards. Such computers are sold with 3 Gb of RAM memory or 6Gb of RAM memory; and are unacceptable.

Computer Hardware. ___

Computers in general are divided into two parts, Hardware and Software. Hardware contains all the major parts of the computer such as the hard drives, The CD/DVD drives, the processors, memory and all the computer input ports such as Printer port, USB port, video port, and keyboard and mouse.

The computer hardware depends on the installed memory, storage drive and processor speed necessary to work with the Windows OS Operating System.

With the hardware and the Windows OS also is important to note the Accessories. Some of these Accessories are built-into the Hardware and

Software. Some of the most important Hardware utilities that are built-in are:

Hardware Security utility; Hardware Management, part of the hardware management is the Command Line CMD.

The hardware System Utilities that includes The Firewall and

Defrag, and the User Utilities that contains the Notepad, WordPad and others.

The Hardware Security Utility contains the **Microsoft Management Console (MMC)** and the hardware Snap-Ins., one of the most important utility built in to allow the user to manage and setup the Security and Configuration of the Computer.

The most important ports on your computer are; the USB ports, most computers will have 2 or more USB ports. USB is a standard that replaces the old computer ports that required large and cumbersome connectors and were very slow sending data back and forth to your computer. USB 2.0 became a defacto standard and was implemented several years ago into every computer hardware. It is very fast sending and receiving data. A USB cable which is thin with the flat USB connector is required to connect almost any device you wish to connect to your computer and it includes cameras, keyboards, Web cams, mouse, etc..

A new USB standard was released last year, its USB 3.0 which is faster than USB2.0 and almost all new computers now have this standard implemented into the hardware. It requires a USB 3.0 cable which is downward compatible to USB2.0

Software.__

Software are the Programs that make all of the Hardware work. The major software in any computer system will be the OS or Operating System such as Windows. The other major software will be the Applications and Utilities. Some software will need to be installed by the user and some will be installed by the OS or Operating System. Major user software will be the Applications such as Microsoft Office, and others that will facilitate the users to become more productive. Utilities will protect the computer from threats and viruses.

Software programs in general are divided into the following areas:
Software Applications, Productivity, Games, Development,
Multimedia, Educational, Utilities, System, LAN Local Area
Networks, Web Software, Maintenance, Network, Paint, Accessories,
Programming, Basic, Communications, Cloud Software, WAN Wide

Area Network (The Internet), Graphics, Antivirus, etc... Software programs are Installed, Deleted, Removed, and Purged.

When a Software program is Installed, it must be Un-Installed.

When a software program is Deleted, it must be Un-Deleted.

To correctly remove Software Programs, it must be done in the Control Panel in Programs and Features, if you are running Windows 8 or **Windows 10.** The program is then Uninstalled or Changed.

Dragging a program to the Trash or Recycle Bin does not Remove it, to Remove a program it must be Shredded in the Recycle Bin.

To Destroy a program it must be Purged.

Most Software are in the following modes, Virtual Software, HyperV Software, Free Software, Search Software, Shared Software, Open
Source Software, Public Domain Software, License Software,
Encrypted Software, Decrypted Software, Cipher Software, Network
Card Test Software or (loop back address Software), OS Windows
Software(Operating Systems); Firewall Software, Security Software(Bit Locker), Printer Software, Email Software, DSL Router Software, etc..

Software Languages and Standards. __

Most Software are written in the following computer languages: Hypertext, used in Web Browsers on the Internet, Unix, Basic, Ada, C and C++ (C Plus Plus), Html (Hypertext Markup Language), Xml (Extensible Markup Language), Fortran, Pascal, and High Level Compilers, etc....like C and C++

The Standards that govern Software are: **Defacto Standards, IEEE Project 802.x, The OSI Model and the ISO (International Standards Organization).**

The Seven Pillars to Execute Software Programs.__

1. Setup and Install the Software
2. Uninstall and Undelete
3. Add and Remove
4. User Install and System Install
5. Run, Search and Delete
6. Free, Trial and Test
7. Open Source and Public Domain software access

Search Software Formats. __

The following Search Software Formats are used on the Internet as follows:

Search with --------→ **AND or +** -------→ Red Cars and Red Vans. Green Apples + Red Apples.

Search with -------→ **OR** ----------→ One word to be in search

(Flight Attendant OR Stewardess.)

Search with ------→ **AND NOT** (-) -→ Suv AND NOT Auto (suv – auto)

Search with ----→ Phrase Searching --→ Exact Phrase within " Harry Potter" Quotation.

Search with ----→ Wildcard ---→ WRIT* CLOU* -→ The Asterisk at the end of words.

Hardware.

The Hardware is the box or frame that contains all the major parts of a computer, the internal hard drive, the CD/DVD Player, the different input ports, the keyboard and mouse, the processor and ram memory, the Ethernet network card, the Wireless network card, the video display, the LCD display(on laptops), the sound card, the internal built in camera, the internal microphone, etc.. One of the major Ports is the USB (Universal Serial Bus) that is now used to connect Printers, Cameras and multiple other devices to your computer hardware.

Policies are built into the computer Hardware to allow for security and to manage the hardware.

Some of the most important policies are the **SECPOL. MSC** (Security Policy) and **GPEDIT. MSC** (Group Policy Editor) these policies allow you to setup the security configuration on your computer hardware. These policies are launched using the Command Line (CMD) built into your computer, or by typing the policy directly into the START or RUN line. The Command Line CMD is provided as a means of accessing your Computer Hardware and Software policies and to directly manage a great part of your computer hardware, without requiring any software to manage policies.

It is used also for direct maintenance of the computer and comes with a reasonable help file. This file contains all of the commands used with the CMD. The command line window when launched appears with a black background. The background and text colors can be changed from a menu of different colors as well as the text size and window size. Some preferred combinations are; red background with yellow text color or green background with white or purple text color, etc… To change the color background and text, click on the cmd icon in the upper left side of the command window.

To access all of the standard policies to set up your computer hardware you can find them in the MMC (Microsoft Management Console) built into your computer hardware.

The MMC allow the user to create SNAP-IN's to setup the hardware and security configuration. To access the MMC just type it into the CMD window or directly into the START or RUN line, on the lower left side of your computer.

CHAPTER 4
CUATRO

Your Computer Hardware Ports and your Desktop. ___

Most computers will have the following standard hardware ports; a printer port, the CD/DVD port, the mouse and keyboard ports, the microphone and audio ports, at least three to four USB ports, the video port, the Ethernet port, the power input port. The USB ports will serve as external ports to connect multiple devices, such as an external Hard Drive or external camera or Webcam.

Your computer hardware ports have *designated hardware symbols* to identify each port. A list of these hardware symbols are contained in this book. Each symbol is imprinted on the external hardware case to identify the port. These symbols meet international standards for hardware identification ports and some have become *"defacto standards."*

Your Desktop. ___

Your Desktop is one of the most important parts of your computer. When you turn on your computer it will boot up and display your desktop window. Your desktop will have a background color or image that can be changed by the user. Your desktop can get corrupted and it is very important to keep your desktop clean from clutter. Having many icons on your desktop will create clutter and take up storage space.

Protected Folders on your Computer._____

Special folders were created to keep your user documents and personal files, in order to keep them organized and off your desktop.

Such folders that are protected are: The *Documents folder*, the *Music folder*, the *Pictures folder*, and the *Videos folder*.

Some icons are required to be on your desktop so that they can be accessible immediately by the user and the system, such as: *My Computer*, *My Network* and *Internet Explorer* or IE.

> If you need to put a copy of documents, pictures or other files you use daily, then you should put them into folders, if they are going to reside on your desktop; and not leave the icon open on your desktop. You could also create *"shortcuts"* of your documents and or applications or any other files you wish to leave on your desktop, instead of leaving the original document or image.
>
> *Shortcuts* do not take up a lot of space or memory. Your desktop icons can be changed in the Control Panel in *"Personalization."*

Laptop Computers vs. Desktop Computers vs. Notebook Computers. ___

Laptop computers were designed to be mobile, containing a battery that would provide from two to four hours of continuing use, and provide all the software and connections necessary to allow the user to work in a wireless environment. Laptops are now fabricated with great processor speeds and large amounts of memory and storage. Desktop computers are the more traditional form of computers built to be fixed in a home or office environment containing very large boxes with many drives and devices. These hardware boxes are generally heavy and are called *"chassis"* and they contain very large power supplies and storage drives that are heavy.

Notebook computers are usually very light and just have a basic operating system designed to provide the most minimum capabilities and connections. They are also limited in processor speed, memory and storage capability. Some notebook computers are now been built with similar capabilities like laptops, with very fast processors. The most popular laptops and notebooks are made by HP (Hewlett Packard), Toshiba, Samsung, and others.

The Task Manager.

Since computers are Task driven machines, and operate by tasks and processes, a Task Manager was built into the OS to manage and organize computer tasks for the user. Sometimes the user will overload the computer with multiple tasks at the same time, and the computer will freeze or crash as it runs out of memory trying to perform all of the tasks requested by the user. Sometimes the users will assume that computers are multitasking machines and they forget that to do multi-tasking, any computer must meet the following minimum criteria:

Must have large amounts of memory (8, 16, or 32 GB)
A very fast processor (Intel dual-core I-5 to I-7 or higher)
A large storage area (500 GB to 1.5 TB) Hard Drive

> The Task Manager will also allow killing a process that hangs causing the computer to freeze, and also allowing the user that is logged on, to " disconnect himself" from the computer without login off.
>
> You can access the Task Manager two ways: From the keyboard, press down at the same time, CTRL+ALT+DEL keys, And also with the CTRL+SHIFT+ESC Keys.
>
> The Task Manager will also show applications that are running, all of the Background processes as well as all of the Windows processes.

It will also show all of the applications that have an impact when your computer startup, and the services that are running in Windows.

The Antivirus Software Program on your Computer._

All computers must have at least a basic Antivirus software program installed on the computer to provide protection against Viruses. Beware of Security programs that are available and claim to protect your computer from viruses, to protect your computer from viruses, you will need to have a full paid version or a basic Free version installed and configured on your computer. The Antivirus Software program should Scan your computer after it has been installed, your computer must be connected to the internet only to get the Virus Definition File Update. The Virus definition File updates your Antivirus program software, so that any known viruses or late published threats, will be known by your Antivirus program, before you run a Scan. Normally after the installation is done your Antivirus program will automatically connect via the internet and update its Definition file before running a Scan.

Once your Antivirus is updated, the next time you run a Scan on your computer; you must be disconnected from the Internet. to disconnect you may turn off your Router or Disable your Ethernet and or Wireless Network Adapters in the Control Panel. Once the scan is completed and no viruses are found, you can re-connect your computer to the Internet or turn back on your Router and or Network Adapter cards.

Run your Antivirus program at least once a week. And keep your Virus Definition File up to date.

Many Antivirus programs exist; the most popular paid versions are made by: Norton, MacAfee, Panda and others.

The Free basic Antivirus that is very popular is made by AVG.

AVG Antivirus can be downloaded from the Internet for free as well as others.

Both the Free versions and the paid versions will provide the protection you need. Do not connect your computer to the Internet if you do not have an Antivirus program installed on your machine. Beware of Trialware Antivirus programs that come with your computer, since they will expire in 30 to 60 days and do not offer any protection to your computer, since they are not a full version of the original software and do not contain all of the software modules. Most of them have no Virus Definition files to update. Most Antivirus programs will not work if their Virus Definition File (**VDF**) is not up to date.

CHAPTER FIVE
CINCO

LIST OF VIRUSES.__

Here is a list of the most common viruses, and what they are: **VIRUS** a program that spreads by replicating itself into other programs or documents **WORM** a self-replicating program, like a Virus, but does not attach itself. It's a self-contained program.

TROJAN a program that appears to be useful, but its not; and contains MALWARE , for example: A Utility

MALWARE Any software program designed to cause harm to your computer.

HOAX VIRUS The worse kind of Virus, it sends hoax messages to users, from the infected computer.

ROOT KITS a very dangerous form of TROJAN, it monitors traffic to and from the infected computer, altering the system files and infecting other computers on the network, without the users knowing.

SPYWARE affects email, and monitors and control part of your computer, by decreasing the computer performance considerable, and infecting your email contacts. **SPAM** a nuisance, not a program and not a threat, its unsolicited mail via email.

Protecting your Computer from Viruses. _____

You can protect your computer by installing a free or paid version of an Antivirus program. Many Antivirus programs are available from different manufacturers, they all protect your computer when properly installed, and with the Virus Definition file updated. A first time Scan is required before the program can begin to protect your computer. Before you start the next Scan, after you have done your first Scan, make sure that you are disconnected from the Internet, and or turn off momentarily your router. Then you may Scan your computer again.

The first time you Scan your computer you need to be connected to the Internet so that your Virus Definition file can get updated.

It is advisable to Scan your computer at least once a week.

A Security software program is not an Antivirus program and does not offer any protection against the many viruses that are a threat. Some Security software programs claim to protect your computer from viruses, only an Antivirus software program will protect your computer from viruses.

Your Computer Security. ___

Windows 7 and 8 comes with some security protection. They are two main security modules in the Control Panel, one of them is called; Windows Defender and the other is Windows Firewall. Make sure that they are both turned on and are working. Your Firewall must be always on to protect your computer from threats.

Firewalls can be internal or external, and can be software and or hardware. Having an external Firewall box will greatly enhance the security protection to your computer.

The Control Panel in Windows 7, 8, 10 . ___

The Control Panel is the heart of your computer. All the modules running in the Control Panel are performing a function so that your computer may run smoothly.

To access the Control Panel, go to the Start or Run button in the lower left side of your Desktop, and select Settings, if the Control Panel is not visible in the menu, to bring up the Control Panel or if you are running Windows 8, 10 you may also go to the Folder on the lower left side of your Desktop, and click on Computer, and the Control Panel will be displayed in the center Tabs that are visible. The Control Panel Icon Folder is unique and very different from any other folders.

Administrative Users vs. Standard Users

In the Control Panel one of the most important controls is the User's Control Panel, where you can Create new Users for your computer and edit existing users. It is recommended that you first create a New User, when you get your computer for the first time. This New User would most likely be you. Once the user is created, you need to give the New User Administrative Rights, so that the user may have full control of the Computer. This user will then become the User Administrator. A Standard User will not have rights and privileges on the computer to do anything. As the Owner of your computer, you need to have full rights on your machine. Otherwise you will not be able to install or remove any software or do basic maintenance on your own machine, so this is a very first most important step, after getting your computer.

System Administrator vs. User Administrator

It is very important to know what is the System Administrator Password. If the Windows System Software gets corrupted, and needs to be re-installed; you will need to know the Administrator Password in order to get into the System to perform general maintenance and re installation of the system software. When Windows is installed for the first time on any machine, in the installation process, a password is requested for the *Administrator,* this password is important to know and remember, if you did not install your system and some one else did it; then you might be out of luck if you do not know the Administrator Password or Admin password. Most computers come with the Windows OS already installed, so the Admin password is not known. It is therefore important to get the original Windows Re installation DVD, so that you may reinstall Windows if it gets corrupted or crashes.

Every new Computer should be provided with the
Installation DVD included in the "sealed" Box and not in a
Box with a Tape over it, which indicates that the Box was opened, and that the original DVD, Manuals and other User Documentation

was taken out. Please note this as it is obvious that the Computer was not shipped to the store in a box with a Tape around it. All Computers are shipped in "sealed" boxes, there is no Tape involved.

The User Administrator only has rights and privileges over the user's machine and does not have any System administrator rights over any of the System software.

If the user tries to change, alter, modify etc.. Any system applications; a message will be displayed alerting the "User" that he or she does not have any rights or privilege to make or do the changes they want.

Please note that the User with Administrative privileges is not the same as the User Administrator.

CHAPTER SIX
SEIS

COMPUTER NETWORKS, NETWORKING AND THE COMPUTER NETWORK CARDS OR ADAPTERS.

Let us define what Computer Networks are first, any computer that is connected to any other computer to share files and other applications is said to be connected to a Network. When computers need to share files and other software they are connected together in a LAN. A LAN is a Local Area Network. To facilitate this configuration, all computers have built in Network Cards or Adapters.

They are two kinds of Network Cards also called NIC's, The first card or NIC is the " **Ethernet Card"** This is a special card that meets the International Standard for Networking called Ethernet **(IEE 802.3)** or Project 802, which is an IEEE Standard, accepted worldwide. The speed of this

network card is 100 Mbps to 1 Gbps.,
(Gigabit Ethernet) or higher.

The Gigabit Ethernet card is much faster than the 100 Mbps card and is desirable.

Wi-Fi WIRELESS CARD OR ADAPTER. _

The second Network card is the Wireless card or WiFi card **(802.11b/g/n)** and the new Standards **ac /ad /ax and x.**

So the built in Wireless card <u>should be</u> (802.11 b/g/n or **802.11 b/g/ac** or **ad**. This is the new Wireless Standard for the Network card that is preferred if you want to have a <u>fast Network connection.</u> If your Wireless card does not meet this standard, then it will be very slow and you will not be able to connect to the Internet. Your Wireless built in card must be at least (802.11 b/g/ac) or higher.

Computers connect to the Internet through these cards. The connection to and from these cards is called **Networking.**

The settings for your Wireless and Ethernet cards are in the Control Panel, and it's called: **"Networking and Sharing Center".**

Networking is divided into LAN (Local Area Networks) and WAN (Wide Area Networks); The largest WAN in the world is the Internet.

Wireless adapters or cards are also installed into Printers which makes them " Wireless Printers" Most printers are now Wireless and require no cables, most printers are supplied with a USB (Universal Serial Bus) Cable, which is another Standard used in computers and networking.

WAN Networking requires special equipment and meets different standards with different kinds of cables and interfaces.

THE NETWORKING MODEL

Networking is based on a Model accepted worldwide; it's called the **OSI Networking** Model or Open Systems Interconnect. Computer Network cards and Networking in general must follow this Model. All network cards are assigned a network protocol number or network ID that identifies the card on the Network. It is a special hexadecimal number (numbers and letters combined), this is also called in networking an IP (Internet Protocol) Address. This IP identifies the computer on a Network and is part of the Internet Protocol (TCP/IP) a Networking Standard. Without a TCP/IP address number the computer can not connect to the Internet or Network.

The speed of the computer Internet connection will depend on the built in Network cards. To find out what kind of Network cards is installed in your computer; go to the
Control Panel to Network and Sharing Center and select **"change adapter settings"** to display the type and kind of network cards installed in the computer.

Networks and the Internet. ____

Networks are used to join computers and devices together and to share resources.

The type of resources that are shared are: Information, Hardware, Software, and Data.

A Hardware resource that is shared could be a single connected Printer, that is shared via the Network to multiple
Computers. These are shared through a LAN (Local Area Network) or a WAN (Wide Area Network.)

To access the Internet services the user can connect via an ISP (Internet Service Provider) or via an OSP (Online Service Provider).

The main Internet Service is the World Wide Web (www.) and **The Internet is the largest Network in the World.**

The Internet is a Worldwide collection of Networks that links individuals with resources and Data. The Internet have Millions of users and is growing more and more every day.
The Web contains Billions of Documents called **Web Pages.**

The Internet Web Page Link. ___

A Web Page on the Internet may link to other Web Documents, and to Text, Graphics, Sound and Video.

A Web site (Google) may contain a collection of related Web Pages. Computers store Web Pages and the user, can use a Web Browser such as IE (Internet Explorer) or Microsoft **Edge**, or **Firefox** to view them.

The content of those Web Pages can be: Financial Data, News, Guides, Weather, Legal Information, other..

A very important Web document or link is: " The Future of Internet 2) a New Technology and Standard for the Internet under Development by the World Wide Web Consortium (wwwc.) or **W3C.**

CHAPTER SEVEN
SIETE

THE INTERNET AND THE WORLD WIDE WEB (WWW).

The Internet is the largest WAN (Wide Area Network) in the world. The internet is managed by the Internet Consortium **(ICANN)** Internet Consortium for Assigned Names and Numbers) and **ISO** International Standard Organization, which regulates standards and Protocols for

the Internet as well as policies. The internet operates with Protocols and Standards that are accepted worldwide.

Computers and Windows consist of three modes for their proper operation; Protocols, Standards and Policies.

Internet Protocols. ___

Protocols are a set of Rules that tell the computer hardware and software how to behave and operate. The Internet uses Protocols to make connections on the Internet and networks, and to regulate the World Wide Web (WWW.)

The Internet Protocols are: http and https (hypertext transport protocol), and www. Or World Wide Web protocol, these protocols must be typed into another protocol called the **URL or Universal Resource Locator.**

The protocol is then displayed as:

http://www. Google.com   As an example.

The Internet Domain. ____

The Internet Domain is considered a major part of the Internet Network. The Internet Network is comprised of the Internet WAN and LAN. The WAN is the Wide Area Network and the LAN is the Local Area Network. Both networks use different types of equipment and Protocols.

The Internet Domain is managed by ICANN Internet Corporation for Assigned Names and Numbers.) this is one of the organizations that Regulates the Internet, and assigns all of the top level domains that are used on the Internet.

The Domain Names or name, is stored in a Server called
DNS or Domain Name Server. This type of High Level Computer is used to translate Domain Names into IP Addresses.

For example; an IP Address that is: 198.80.146.30 once translated by the DNS, becomes the Domain Name: www.scsite.com

The Web address and Web Page of an Internet site would be written as:
http://www.nmsu.edu/careers/index.html
Where, http:// is the Protocol, the Domain name is, www.nmsu.edu the Path is careers and index.html is the **Web Page Name.**

The Internet was developed in 1960 and the World Wide Web (www.) in 1990.
The Internet is identified as: " A World Wide Collection of Electronic Documents called a Web Page.
A " Web Browser" is the Application Software to access " Web Pages".

The Top Level Domains used on the Internet are:

.COM, .EDU, .BIZ, .INFO, .GOV, .MIL, .NAME, .PRO,
.NET, .ORG, .AERO, and .COOP

Using the Internet. _____

To use the Internet, computers require a Web Application called a "Browser" such as IE Internet Explorer, or Firefox.
They are several Browsers available for use on the Internet.
The most popular ones are, Internet Explorer, Firefox,
Opera, Safari, etc.. A **Web Page** is created for each Web Application, for example; you can use Firefox as your Web Browser with Google as your Web Page.

> The Internet begins by starting a service called " Internet
> Service," when Windows 7 or 8 start up., then running the
> Application software or Browser, to allow the user to view
> Web Sites on the World Wide Web and their respective Web

Pages. A very popular Web Browser is IE or Internet
Explorer developed by Microsoft., other popular Web Browsers are Firefox, developed by Mozilla and Safari developed by Apple Computers. Other Web Browsers are available on the Internet, and can be downloaded for free.

Each Web Page address will be displayed in the Web address URL (Universal Resource Locator) window.

In this window is where the Protocol HTTP: or HTTPS: should be typed, followed by the symbol // and the words: WWW. (World Wide Web) followed by the Internet address; for example: http://www.nmsu.edu/index.html

The http is the Protocol, which stands for: Hypertext Transport Protocol, and www. Is also a Protocol that identifies the world wide web. The www.nmsu.edu is called the " Domain" and index.html displays the Web Page Name. All Web Pages are displayed by their Index, and html (Hypertext Markup Language) is the Computer Language used to develop the index and Web Pages.

Some Web Pages are also developed using another language called XML (Extensible Markup Language).

Free Web Browser Plug-Ins. _____

To extend the capability of your Web Browser, you may install one or more **" Plug-Ins "** that will enhance the display of Multimedia Elements on the Web Page you are viewing. Some of the Free Plug-Ins available on the Internet for downloading are the following: Acrobat Reader, to view .pdf files on the Internet, or secure documents created with Acrobat in .pdf file format. **FlashPlayer, from Macromedia.com,** to view Graphic Animation on the Internet. , **LiquidPlayer from liquidaudio.com** to play Audio CD and MP3 audio files, RealOnePlayer, from Real.com to play and view live audio and video on the internet., Quicktime, from Apple.com to play HD Music audio and video on the Internet.; **ShockwavePlayer, from Macromedia.com** to play and view Multimedia 3D Graphics with HD audio and video, supporting Dolby 6.1 or higher and Surround Sound Formats.

Important Search Engines. ___

The software program contained in most Web Pages all have built in " Search Engines". The search engines are necessary for the user to be able to find what he or she is looking for. Some search engines will use the IP address or Internet Protocol Address, to search Web Sites and or Web Pages to find the information requested. Some Web Pages may contain one or more Search Engines.

The following are very important search engines on the
Internet: HotBot.com, Excite.com, AlltheWeb.com,
Altavista.com, AskJeeves.com, Lycos.com, LookSmart.com,
Webcrawler.com, Overture.com, Infospace.com, etc…

Graphic Formats used on the Internet. ___

The following Graphic Formats are used on the **WWW**.
And are: **.png** (Portable Network Graphics); **.gif** (
Graphic Interchange Format); **.bmp** (Bitmap); **.pcx** (PC Paintbrush); **.jpeg**

(Joint Photographic Experts Group); **.tiff** (Tagged Image File Format).

Internet Protocol Address (IP.) uses the form: 198.80.146.30 or for example: 207.46.197.113 Which is equal to Microsoft Address: www.microsoft.com

207.46.197 identifies the Internet Network, and 113 identifies the Computer.

INTERNET WEB ADDRESSES vs. EMAIL ADDRESSES. __

Web addresses are different from Email addresses as they must contain the full Web Protocol, and is displayed as: http://www.nmsu.edu

Email addresses are different as they only display the user name and At sign or @ with the ISP (Internet Service Provider) and is displayed as: johndoe@ yahoo.com or marydoe@hotmail.com

Standards.__

Standards are required on the Internet and all Computer Hardware and Software. The responsibility on these standards falls on an organization called ISO or International Standards Organization. This organization makes, changes, creates and modifies all standards for hardware and software. Standards are then divided into Proprietary, **Defacto,** National and International Standards, etc.. Some standards are open and accepted worldwide and becomes " defacto standards", such as HP standards for their Printers and other devices, and are **HPGL** (Hewlett Packard Graphic Language), **PDL,** Postscript Description Language, **PDF** Postscript Description File, etc..

Policies.___

Policies govern both hardware and software. Computer policies let the user's change the way computers behave and allow the users to modify the computer hardware to provide security on their system. An example is the Group Policy Editor or (GPEDIT.msc) a Microsoft Policy Editor and (SECPOL. msc) a Security Policy to set up your computer.

Microsoft Management Console MMC and SNAP-INS. ____

The Microsoft Management Console or MMC is built into every computer running Windows, and provides policies and rules and regulations that are user friendly and allows the users to modify and change how some parts of their computers should operate, by turning on and or shutting down services that are not needed or required in Windows OS. To see the available policies and other software, type into the search area by the start button, the command: MMC to bring up the Microsoft Management Console. The MMC allows the user to create SNAPINS, small utility programs that allow the user to manage, clean and secure his computer. Many SNAPINS are already included in the MMC to use right away.

After typing MMC into the Start or Run window on the lower left side of the computer desktop, the MMC Console window will be displayed, just select " add or remove snapins" to view and or select the snapin you want to work with, or use the following step by step procedure:

The Microsoft Management Console (MMC) let users create much more flexible user interfaces and customize administration tools.

MMC unifies and simplifies day-to-day system management tasks. It hosts tools and displays them as consoles. These tools, consisting of one or more applications, are built with modules called snap-ins. The snap-ins also can include additional extension snap-ins. MMC is a core part of Microsoft's management strategy and is included in Microsoft Windows® operating systems. In addition, Microsoft development groups will use MMC for future management applications.

Microsoft Management Console enables system administrators and users to create special tools to delegate specific administrative tasks to users or groups. Microsoft provides standard tools with the operating system that perform everyday administrative tasks that users need to accomplish. These are part of the **All Users** profile of the computer and located in the **Administrative Tools** group on the **Startup** menu. Saved as MMC console (.msc) files, these custom tools can be sent by e-mail, shared in a network folder, or posted on the Web. They can also be assigned to users, groups, or computers with system policy settings. A tool can be scaled up and down, integrated seamlessly into the operating system, repackaged, and customized.

Using MMC, system administrators can create unique consoles for workers who report to them or for workgroup managers. They can assign a tool with a system policy, deliver the file by e-mail, or post the file to a shared location on the network. When a workgroup manager opens the .msc file, access will be restricted to those tools provided by the system administrator.

Building your own tools with the standard user interface in MMC is a straightforward process. Start with an existing console and modify or add components to fulfill your needs. Or create an entirely new console. The following example shows how to create a new console and arrange its administrative components into separate windows.

Prerequisites and Requirements

There are no prerequisites: you don't need to complete any other step-bystep guide before starting this guide. You need one computer running either Windows 2000, Windows XP, Windows 7 or Windows 8. For the most current information about hardware requirements and compatibility for servers, clients, and peripherals, see the Check Hardware and Software Compatibility page on the Windows website.

Creating Consoles

The most common way for administrators to use MMC is to simply start a predefined console file from the Start menu. However, to get an idea of the flexibility of MMC, it is useful to create a console file from scratch. It is also useful to create a console file from scratch when using the new task delegation features in this version of MMC.

Creating a New Console File (SNAP-IN)

1. On the Start Menu, click **Run**, type **MMC**, and then click **OK**. Microsoft Management Console opens with an empty console (or administrative tool) as shown in Figure 1 below. The empty console has no management functionality until you add some snap-ins. The MMC menu commands on the menu bar at the top of the

Microsoft Management Console window apply to the entire console.

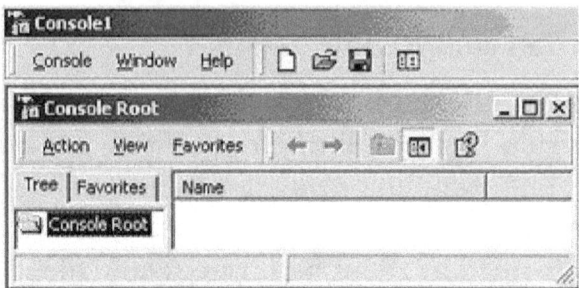

Figure 1: Beginning Console Window Click Console (under Console1). On the Console Menu, click Add/Remove Snap-in. The Add/Remove Snap-in dialog box opens. This lets you enable extensions and configure which snapins are in the console file. You can specify where the snap-ins should be inserted in the Snap-in's "added to drop-down box." Accept the default, Console Root, for this exercise.

Click **Add**. This displays the Add Standalone Snap-in dialog box that lists the snap-ins that are installed on your computer.

From the list of snap-ins, double-click **Computer Management** to open the **Computer Management** wizard.

5. Click **Local computer** and select the check box for "**Allow the selected computer to be changed when launching from the command line.**" Click Finish. This returns you to the Add/Remove Snap-ins dialog box. Click Close.

Click the **Extensions** tab as shown in Figure 2 below. By selecting the check box **Add all extensions**, all locally-installed extensions on the computer are used. If this check box is not selected, then any extension snap-in that is selected is explicitly loaded when the console file is opened on a different computer.

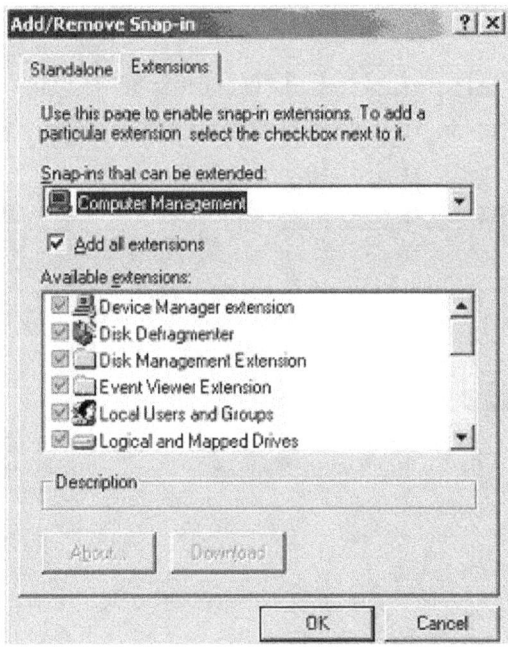

Figure 2: Select All Extensions

8. Click **OK** to close the Add/Remove Snap-in dialog box. The Console Root window now has a snap-in, **Computer Management**, rooted at the Console Root folder.

Customizing the Display of <u>Snap-ins in the Console</u>: New Windows

After you add the snap-ins, you can add windows to provide different administrative views in the console.
To add windows

1. In the left pane of the tree view in Figure 3 below, click the **+** next to **Computer Management**. Click **System Tools**.

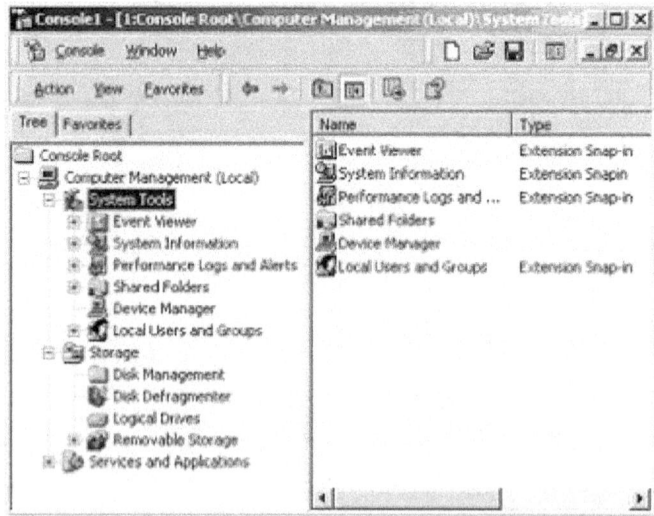

Figure 3: Console1: System Tools

2. Right-click the **Event Viewer** folder that opens, and then click **New window** from here. As shown in Figure 4 below, this opens a new Event Viewer window rooted at the Event Viewer extension to computer management.

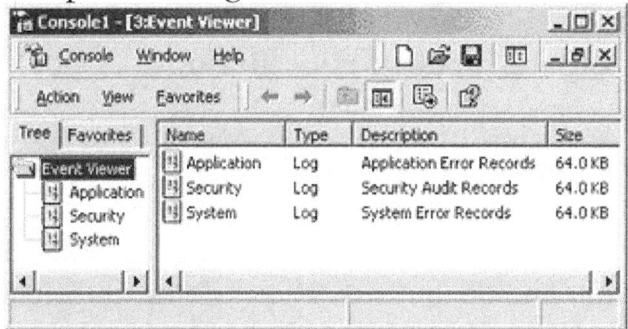

Figure 4: Event Viewer

Click **Window** and click **Console Root**.

In the Console Root window, click **Services and Applications**, right-click **Services** in the left pane, and then click **New Window**. As shown in Figure 5 below, this opens a new Services window rooted at the Event Viewer extension to Computer Management. In the new window, click the **Show/Hide Console Tree** toolbar button to hide the console tree, as shown in the red circle in Figure 5 below.

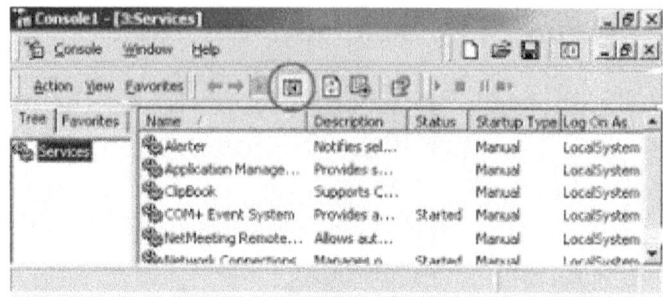

Figure 5: Show/Hide Button

Close the original window with Console Root showing in it.

On the Window menu, select **Tile Horizontally**. The console file should appear and include the information shown in Figure 4 and Figure 5 above.

You can now save your new MMC console. Click the **Save as** icon on the Console window, and give your console a name. Your console is now saved as a .msc file, and you can provide it to anyone who needs to configure a computer with these tools.

Note: Each of the two smaller windows has a toolbar with buttons and drop-down menus. The toolbar buttons and drop-down menus on these each of these two windows apply only to the contents of the window. You can see that a window's toolbar buttons and menus change depending on the snap-in selected in the left pane of the window. If you select the View menu, you can see a list of available toolbars.

Tip: The windows fit better if your monitor display is set to a higher resolution and small font.

Creating Console Taskpads

If you are creating a console file for another user, it's useful to provide a very simplified view with only a few tasks available. Console taskpads help you to do this.

To create a console taskpad

From the Window menu, select **New Window**. Close the other two windows (you will save a new console file at the end of this procedure). Maximize the remaining window. In the left pane, click the **+** next to the **Computer Management** folder, then click the **+** next to the **System Tools** folder. Click **System**, click the **Event Viewer** folder, right-click **System**, and select **New Taskpad** View.

Go through the wizard accepting all the default settings. Verify the checkbox on the last page is checked so that the Task Creation wizard can start automatically.

Choose the defaults in the Task Creation wizard until you come to the page shown below in Figure 6, then choose a list view task and select **Properties**:

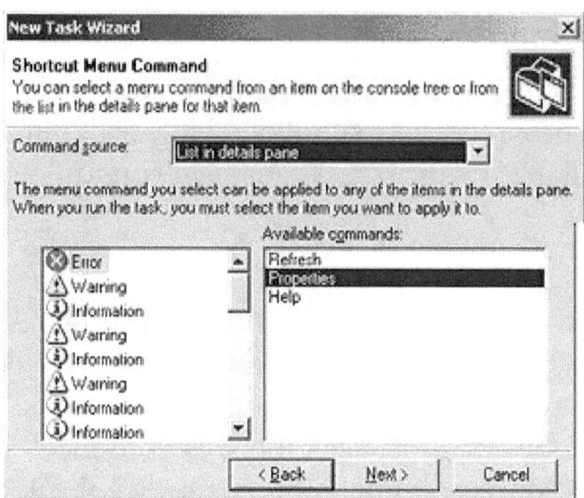

Figure 6: New Task Wizard

Click **Next** and accept the defaults for the rest of the screens. By selecting an Event and clicking **Properties**, you can see the property page for that Event.

After you click **Finish** on the last screen, your console should look like Figure 7 below:

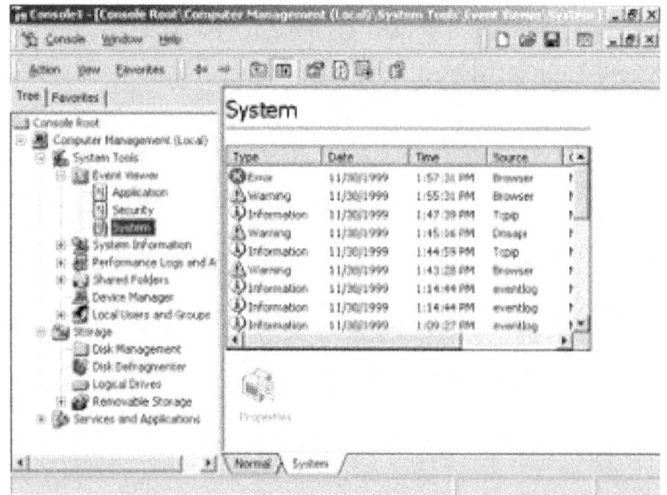

Figure 7: New Console Showing System Event Log

Click the **Show/Hide console tree** toolbar button.

From the view menu, click **Customize** and click each of the options except the Description bar to hide each type of toolbar.

The next section discusses how to lock the console file down so that the user sees only a limited view. For right now your console file should look like Figure 8 below.

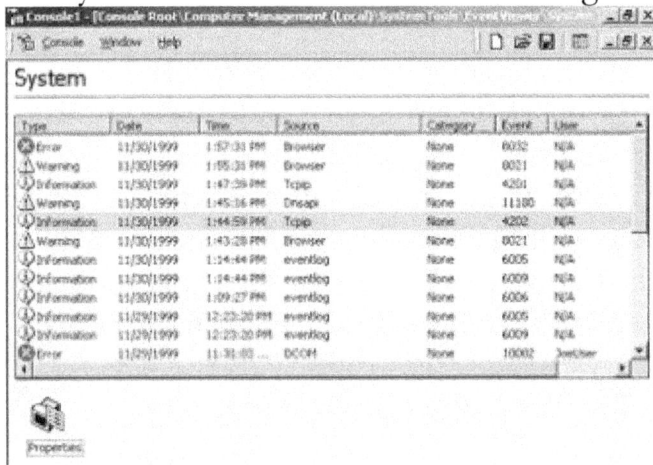

Figure 8: Customized View

Setting Console File Options

If you are creating a console file for another user, it is useful to prevent that user from further customizing the console file. The Options dialog box allows you to do this.

To set console file options

From the **Console** menu, select **Options**. Change the Console Mode by selecting **User Mode limited access, single window** from the drop-down dialog box. This will prevent a user from adding new snap-ins to the console file or rearranging the windows. You can change the name from Console1. Click **OK** to continue.

Save the console file. The changes will not take effect until the console file is opened again.

This is just one example of how the Microsoft Management Console lets you group information and functionality that previously would have required opening a Control Panel option plus two separate administrative tools. The modular architecture of MMC makes it easy for users to create snap-in Applications that leverage the platform while easing administrative load.

Built In MMC Snap-Ins.

Microsoft has based most of its management applications on the Microsoft Management Console (MMC). The MMC provides a framework for building management consoles. Microsoft and many thirdparty application vendors have used this framework for creating their management consoles.

The MMC uses snap-ins for system and application management. Windows 7 & 8 comes with many built-in MMC snap-ins you can use to manage the system. You can use them to manage user settings, Windows applications, security, and many other vital aspects of the system.

Windows 7 & 8 contains the following built-in **MMC** snap-ins:**ActiveX Control** – You can add individual ActiveX controls to view and configure. These Internet Explorer plug-ins add functionality to the browser.

Authorization Manager – You can set permissions for Authorization Manager-enabled applications.

Certificates – You can configure different certificate stores available on the system. Certificates help provide a secure operating environment. You can use them for identification, securing data and securing communications. There are certificate stores for users, applications, and the system itself.**Component Services** – You can manage the system's COM+, or Component Services configuration. You can also configure Distributed

> Computer Object Model (DCOM) and Distributed Transaction Coordinator (DTC) settings. These are especially important when programs need to communicate between multiple computers.**Computer Management** – This is actually a collection of snapins used for task scheduling, disk management, performance monitoring, and many other configuration and management tasks.**Device Manager** – This is for viewing and configuring

hardware installed on the system. You can disable devices, update drivers and troubleshoot potential issues.

Disk Management – This is for disk and volume management.

You can create volumes, format disks and enable fault tolerance.

Event Viewer – This is for viewing system event logs that help you determine if your system or applications are having problems. You can also use the Security log to determine if there has been unauthorized access.**Folder** – This is to add a folder for organizing your snap-ins, which comes in handy if you've added numerous snap-ins to a single MMC console.**Group Policy Object Editor** – This lets you configure the Group Policy Objects on the system.

IP Security Monitor – This helps you monitor the status of your IP Security (IPsec) configuration, which secures communication between computers.

 IP Security Policy Management – This helps you understand and configure the settings in your IPsec policy.

Link to Web Address – This lets you add a Web page to the MMC, which can be useful for applications and systems with Webbased management.

Local Users and Groups – This lets you configure users and groups on the local system, add user accounts, delete user accounts and configure various user properties.

NAP Client Configuration – This lets you configure Network Access Protection (NAP) client configuration settings.

Performance Monitor – This lets you monitor your system performance, including memory, hard disks, processors and a number of other components.

Print Management – This helps you manage print servers and printers connected to the system.

Resultant Set of Policy – This shows you what settings will be applied by your Group Policy settings, without actually applying them to the system.

Security Configuration and Analysis – This analyzes your configuration and security templates.

Security Templates – This lets you edit the security templates you applied to your system.

Services – This lets you view and configure properties for services running on the system. You can disable, start, stop or restart services; configure authentication and fault tolerance.

Shared Folders – This lets you view properties and status information for file shares. You can see what folders are being shared and who's accessing them.

Task Scheduler – This lets you schedule tasks to be automatically run at specified times or at specified intervals.

TPM Management – This lets you configure the Trusted Platform Module, which generates keys for cryptographic operations.

Windows Firewall with Advanced Security – This lets you configure Windows Firewall settings to control what processes, applications, and systems can access your system or generate network traffic from your system.

WMI Control – This lets you configure and manage the Windows Management Instrumentation (WMI) service, for managing and monitoring Windows systems.

CHAPTER EIGHT
OCHO

Application Software and Support Tools. ____

Several Application Software and Support tools are available to the user. Most of these tools are built into the applications and or Windows Operating Systems (OS) and are: Online Help, User Manual, Web Based Help, Wizards, such as the Memo Wizard; and Links to Websites that contain FAQ (Frequently Asked Questions and Chat Rooms.

Most Windows applications may contain support tools for Digital
Video and Windows Movie Maker as well as tools to show audio
and video compressed and stored files, and allow the user to choose Codec and to transfer Video from a Camera.

The following file formats are chosen sometimes by the System automatically or by the user:
Apple Quicktime Formats (.mov and .qt); Microsoft Windows
Media Player (.wmv and .asf); RealNetworks Realmedia (.rm and

.ram). These formats are used by the application or the user to Encode Audio and Video.

The seven Pillars of Software Applications. ___

Seven Software steps exist to guide the user through the process of setting up any software.

The software process starts first with the " Setup and Install of the Application itself"., The User Install and the System Install, then we have the "Uninstall and Undelete" and the " Add and Remove", then the " Run and Delete", " The Free and Trial " and the " Open Source and Public Domain".

Software is divided into: Freeware Software, Trialware Software, Open Source Software and Public Domain Software.

All of these different types of Software can be obtained Free.

These types of Software are available for download from the Internet for free.

Multimedia Software and Applications. __

Many types of Multimedia and Windows Software Applications exist, the most important ones are:

Printing Applications, Game Applications, Word Processing Applications, Microsoft Office Applications, Multimedia Applications, Drawing and Painting Applications, Network Applications. Under Word Processing
Applications we have " Microsoft Word", Notepad and Word Pad to help the user write a simple letter or a more professional letter. Under Office Applications we have " Microsoft Office" and the Free Office Application " Open Office".

Under Drawing and Painting Applications, we have Paint, Adobe Illustrator, Adobe Photoshop, Adobe Premier, and Adobe Acrobat.
Under Network Applications, we have Port Scanner, and Network
Monitor. Under Multimedia Applications, we have Windows Media Player, with CD/DVD Burner Software and Nero Software, that also read and burn CD's and Dvd's.

Windows Software Organization. __

Windows Software is organized into the following types of Software:
Antivirus, Development, Lan, Games, Graphics, Wan, Cloud,
Communications, Accessories, Utilities, Applications, Productivity, Multimedia, Programming, Basic, Paint, Web, Maintenance, Network, System, Server,

Educational, Virtual, Hyper-V, Windows OS, Firewall, Security, Printer, and Email.

All of these Software types can be Installed, Deleted, Removed, Purged, Uninstalled, Undeleted, Shredded, and Destroyed.

The software can also be Shared, Open Source, Free, Public Domain, License, Encrypted, Decrypted, and Cypher protected.

Two special Software Tests are used: The Network Card or Adapter Test, and the DSL Router Test.

The Network Adapter Card Test is called the " loopback test" and it is performed by the user. Use the command " Ping" with **127.0.0.1** typed into the Command Line CMD. (ping 127.0.0.1) On the Computer, or just type it into the "start" window, on the lower left side of the Computer.

The DSL Router Test is done the same way, but using the address: 192.168.0.1 or 192.168.1.1 typed into the URL window of the Web Page that is been used on the Internet. Can be IE (Internet Explorer) or Firefox.

Software is developed from different computer languages, which are: HyperText, Basic, ADA, Unix, C and C++, Html, Xml, Low Level Languages like Fortran, Pascal, Cobol, and or High Level Compilers, like C and C++.

Software Standards. __

Software Standards are regulated by ISO International Standards Organization, IEEE (Project 802.x), Defacto, Network (OSI Model), and others.

When Software Applications do not work.__

In the case of Antivirus Application Software, the Antivirus Software can be Free or Licensed. The Software need to be Updated periodically by using " Update Now" or "Live Update" to update the " Virus Definition" File. If this file is not updated to the current definitions, the Software will not work. The Virus Definition, updates itself with the latest Viruses reported and any new Virus that is reported in the community.

CHAPTER NINE
NUEVE

Creating the " All Applications Folder". __

The All Applications Folder is created by the user, on the Computer Desktop. Right Click on any part of the Desktop and select New, and " Shortcut" from the menu. When the shortcut window is displayed, type in the location of the item:
Explorer Shell:AppsFolder and click Next to continue.

Type the name of this shortcut, for example: ALL APPLICATIONS, and click **Finish** to create the shortcut **as displayed below.**

You may call this folder by any name you prefer, however the purpose will be to have a single folder

```
Create Shortcut

What item would you like to create a shortcut for?

This wizard helps you to create shortcuts to local or network programs, files, folders, comp
Internet addresses.

Type the location of the item:
Explorer Shell:AppsFolder                                          Browse

Click Next to continue.

                                                                    Next
```

on the desktop that contains all of the installed applications on the computer, regardless of their location in the All Programs section of the Windows system.

The All Applications folder will be created. This folder will look different from any other folder on the desktop.
An example is displayed below.

Name the ShortCut, and click Finish, to create the special Folder.

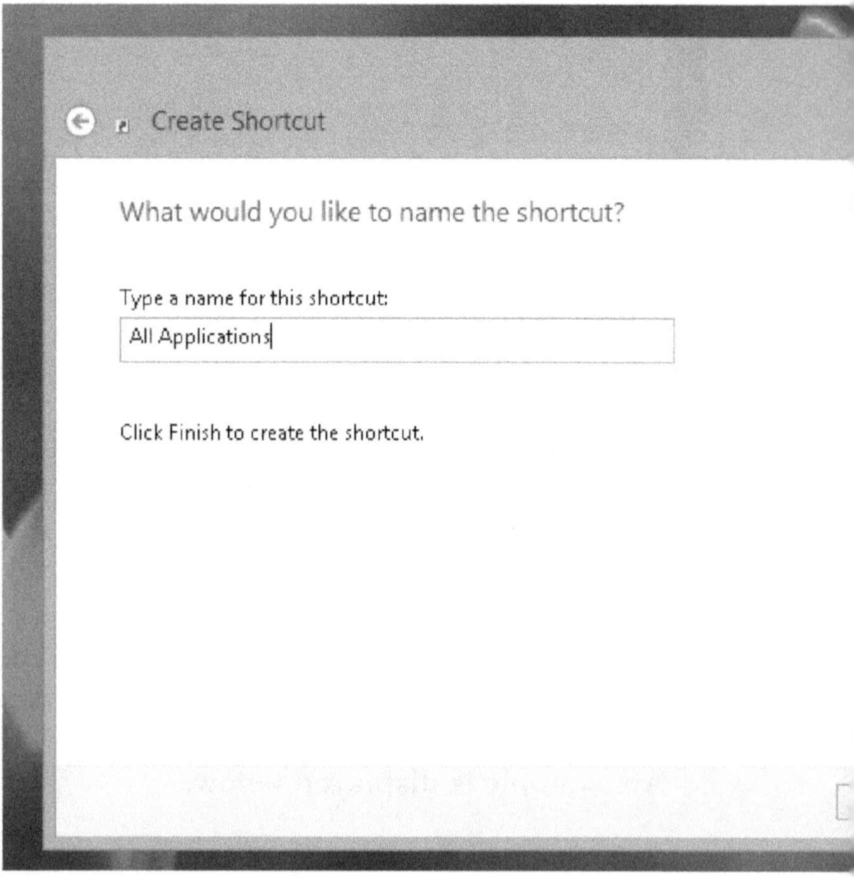

The All Applications folder will contain all of the applications installed on the computer, more than what is displayed in the Computer. You will be able to see and display more than 166 items installed on the computer by the system and those installed by the user.

The advantage is that all those applications will be able to launch immediately, bypassing the all programs section of the computer.

They will launch very fast and will not require any "loading" by the system.

Creating the " Advantage" or Magic Folder. __

The Advantage folder is a very unique folder that can be created on the desktop. It requires typing an exact code after creating a New Folder on the desktop.

It is very important to remember to **put a Period** after the new folder is given a name, which can be " Magic." or "Advantage." or any name the user prefers, that identifies the content of the folder.

The folder will contain a tabulated and very organized list of over 200 items that covers every section of the Computer and how to troubleshoot that section and or specific instructions on what to do to fix the problem or problems you may encounter.

Start by creating a new folder on the desktop. Right click and select New from the Menu to create a New Folder. The New Folder will be created. Give the New Folder a name, for example: Magic. Or Advantage.

For example: **Advantage.{ (open bracket)** type in Code….. **(close bracket}** then press <Enter> and the New Advantage Folder will be created.

This folder will look completely different from any other folder on the desktop including the All Applications folder.

Once the folder is created, you may double click on it to open the folder and display all of the tabulated files and menu's.

Enter the following Code exactly with the period after the folder and dashes after the numbers, after you name the folder:

Advantage.{ED7BA470-8E54-465E-825C-99712043E01C} press Enter.

The Advantage folder will be created. See examples below.

The Advantage Folder Created, will look like this:

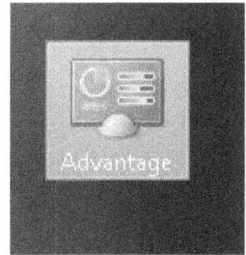

These are some of the Files in the Advantage folder:

Notice that they are Tabulated by sections in the computer and the folder contains 256 items... Each section like the "Action Center" displayed; contains 18 different items that you can do and or troubleshoot in this section. Other sections of the computer will contain more items.

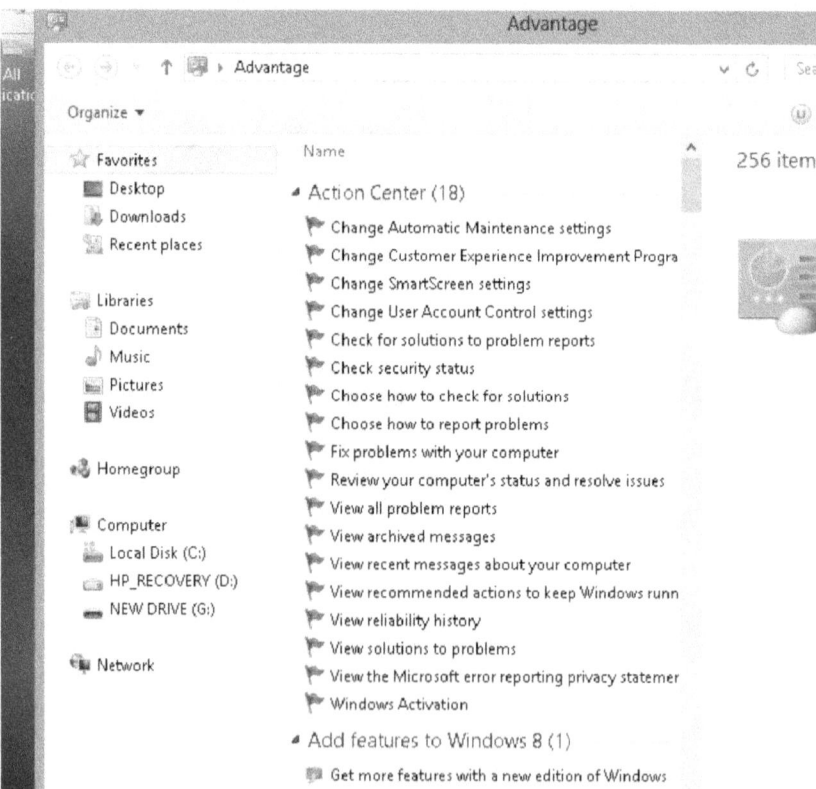

This unique folder will contain information and instructions on how to Navigate your Computer in Windows 7, 8, and 10., and how to perform

Diagnostics on your computer, the use of Quick Access Menus, How to boot into Safe Mode, how to install Plug Ins on your computer, monitoring your computer temperature, using a Word processor, using Narrator to read your documents,using Microsoft Office Applications, saving your work files, using paint applications, how to Calibrate your computer colors, setting up your Email, using Multimedia Applications, using the Internet, how to monitor and test your network and adapter cards, how to setup your wireless network, and how to clean and protect your computer with utilities., and many more items.

Use a Flashdrive as Memory with Ready Boost.

Ready Boost will work better on Computers with low RAM or Memory, from 2 GB, to 4 GB. Aprox.

Ready Boost is built into every computer running Windows 8 operating System. To access Ready Boost, go to Computer or My Computer and select your Flashdrive that you just connected to your USB port. You may use any USB Port on your computer.

The Flashdrive that will be used should be at least 4 Gb Gigabytes or higher. Eight (8) Gigabytes capacity is preferred. Only 4094 Bytes (4 GB minimum) is recommended to dedicate for Ready Boost.

Once you select your Flashdrive, right click it to select Properties.

Select the Ready Boost Tab

Check" Dedicate this device to Ready Boost"

Select the " space to reserve for system speed"

Windows recommends reserving 4094 Bytes for best results;

Click on Apply, then

<ok> Restart the

Computer.

Your Flashdrive will now be dedicated with Ready Boost as more additional memory, and the computer should run faster.

Using the Built in Diagnostics for your Computer.

A complete set of Diagnostics Tools are built into Windows for the user to troubleshoot, as well as other hidden tools.

To use the built in Diagnostics, type into the search box on the lower left corner of the desktop, the words:
DXDiag

This will bring up the Direct X Diagnostic Tool.

With four Tabs, System, Display, Sound and Input. This will give the user a Report of each of these sections on the computer and note if any problems are found or detected.

It is a good idea to run this tool periodically if you suspect that the Computer is not working correctly. This is a tool the user can access at any time.

The Quick Access Menu Tool. ____

The Quick Access menu Tool is one of the other tools available to the user. To access this tool, hold down the " Windows Key" on your Keyboard and press the X key. This key is located on the lower left side of the keyboard, beside the ALT key and has a Symbol of a Flag on top of it.

The Quick Access menu will Display 16 Items to allow the user to navigate to these sections of the computer very quickly.

The Defragment and Optimize Drive Tool. __

This built-in tool allow the user to Defragment the drives on the computer and Optimize the drives as well.

To access this tool, just type into the search window on the lower left side of the computer, the words: DEFR and the Defragment window will be displayed. Select the " Defragment Drives and Optimize".

You may set the tool to Optimize the Drives on the computer automatically when the Tool is displayed.

The tool will show the drives on the computer and their status. The drives will be analyzed first before they are optimized.

The Calibrate your Screen Tool. ___

The Windows built-in Calibrate Tool allows the user to calibrate the Computer Screen. To access the tool just type into the Search box on the lower left side of the computer the words: DCCW

The Display Color Calibration Window will be displayed. Just follow the instructions.

The Shutdown Tool in Windows 8. ___

One of the other built in tools available to the user is the " Shutdown Tool" in Windows 8. This Tool provides a correct and alternate way to properly shutdown the computer.

To access this tool, hold down the ALT key and press the F4 function Key, located on the first row of the keyboard.

This will display the shutdown window, that is displayed below:

> The Windows shutdown window will allow the user to shutdown correctly and quickly as well as other things by selecting the arrow in the shutdown window. To Shutdown Windows, just click on OK.

WINDOWS 8 HOTKEYS.

Win key - Toggles between Start Screen and Windows Desktop

Win+X - Opens Quick Access Menu as

mentioned in point 1

Win+PrntScr - Automatically saves screenshot in Pictures folder as mentioned in point 2

Win+C - Shows Charms Bar

Win+D – Open Desktop

Win+I - Shows Settings panel

Win+K - Launches Devices charm

Win+H - Launches Share charm

Win+Q - Launches Search charm

Win+W - Launches Settings search page

Win+F - Launches Files search page

Win+Tab - Shows Metro apps switcher as mentioned in point 4

Win+Z - Shows / hides App bar at Start Screen to show all apps

Win+Spacebar - Toggles between input languages and keyboard layout

Win+, - From Start Screen peeks at the Desktop

Win+Enter - Launches Narrator

Ctrl+F1 - Minimizes / maximizes ribbon in Windows Explorer

Ctrl+Tab – Launches All Apps list on Start Screen

Ctrl+Shift+N- To create a New Folder quickly

Fn+prtsc - Copy screen

Alt+F4 – Close Application – Shutdown

NOTES

NOTES

CHAPTER TEN
DIEZ

Basic Computer Terms

CPU
> *Central processing unit*; the brain of the computer; controls the other elements of the computer

Disk Drive
> A peripheral device that reads and/or writes information on a disk

Hard Drive
> A device (usually within the computer case) that reads and writes information, including the operating system, program files, and data files

Keyboard
> A peripheral used to input data by pressing keys

Modem
> A peripheral device used to connect one computer to another over a phone line

Monitor
> A device used to display information visually

Mouse
> A peripheral device used to point to items on a monitor

NIC
> *Network interface card*; a board inserted in a computer that provides a physical connection to a network

Printer
> A peripheral device that converts output from a computer into a printed image

Software

Applications
> Complete, self-contained programs that perform a specific function (ie. spreadsheets, databases)

Bit
> A computer's most basic unit of information that represents zero
> (0) or one (1)

Boot
> The process of loading or initializing an operating system on a computer; usually occurs as soon as a computer is turned on

Browser
> A program used to view World Wide Web pages, such as
> Netscape Navigator or Internet Explorer

Bug

> A part of a program that usually causes the computer to malfunction; often remedied in patches or updates to the program

Byte
> Small unit of data storage; 8 bits; usually holds one character, 8 bits equal 1 byte

Click
> Occurs when a user presses a button on a mouse which in turn, generates a command to the computer

Database
> A large structured set of data; a file that contains numerous records that contain numerous fields

Diskette
> A small flexible disk used for storing computer data

Double Click
> Occurs when a user presses a button on the mouse twice in quick succession; this generates a command to the computer

Download
> Transferring data from another computer to your computer

Drag
> Occurs when a user points the mouse at an icon or folder, presses the button and without releasing the button, moves the icon or folder to another

place on the computer where the button is released

Driver
: Software program that controls a piece of hardware or a peripheral

FAQ
: *Frequently asked question*; documents that answer questions common to a particular website or program

File
: Namable unit of data storage; an element of data storage; a single sequence of bytes

Folder
: A graphical representation used to organize a collection of computer files; as in the concept of a filing cabinet (computer's hard drive) with files (folders)

Freeware
: Software provided at no cost to the user

Gigabyte
: 1,073,741,824 bytes or 1,024 megabytes; generally abbreviated GB

GUI
: *Graphical user interface*; uses pictures and words to represent ideas, choices, functions, etc.

Icon
> A small picture used to represent a file or program in a GUI interface

Internet
> A network of computer networks encompassing the World Wide
> Web, FTP, telnet, and many other protocols

IP number
> *Internet protocol*; a computer's unique address or number on the Internet

Kilobyte
> 1,024 bytes; usually abbreviated

KB Megabyte
> 1,048,576 bytes or 1,024 kilobytes; enough storage to approximately equal a 600 page paperback book; generally abbreviated Mb

Memory
> Any device that holds computer data

Menu
> A list of operations available to the user of a program

Network
> A collection of computers that are connected

Peripheral
> Any of a number of hardware devices connected to a CPU

RAM
: *Random access memory*; the type of storage that changes; when the computer is turned off, the RAM memory is erased

ROM
: *Read-only memory*; the type of storage that is not changed even when the computer is turned off

Scroll Bar
: Allows the user to control which portion of the document is visible in the window; available either horizontally or vertically or both

Shareware
: Software provided at a minimal cost to users who are on their honor to send in payment to the programmer

Spreadsheet
: A program arranged in rows and columns that manipulates numbers

Tool Bar
: A graphical representation of program activities; a row of icons used to perform tasks in a program

URL
: *Universal or Uniform resource locator*; the address of a site on the World Wide Web; a standard way of locating objects on the Internet

Virus
: A deliberately harmful computer program designed to create annoying glitches or destroy data

Window
: A screen in a software program that permits the user to view several programs at one time

Word Processor
: A program that allows the user to create primarily text documents

Wi-Fi
: Wireless Network standard 802.11 a/b/g/n for Wireless Network Adapters

Application Files
Program files environment where you can create and edit the kind of document that application makes.

Click
To select an object by pressing the mouse button when the cursor is pointing to the required menu option, icon or hypertext link.

Close
To close a window that has been opened for viewing and / or editing.

Computer

A general-purpose machine that processes data according to a set of instructions that are stored internally either temporarily or permanently.

Central Processor Unit (CPU)

This term has two meanings (just to confound beginners, you understand) 1) Central Processor Unit--the main chip on the computer that makes everything go.
2) The box that holds the guts of the computer.
A faster CPU is always better than a slower one. You can never have too fast of a CPU.

Crash

Your computer or application no longer works correctly and so you "loose" all the work you've done since the last time you saved.

Creating A File

Storing data as a file with an assigned file name that is unique within the directory it resides in.

Delete

To remove an item of data from a file or to remove a file from the disk.

Desktop

An on-screen representation of a desktop such as used in the Macintosh and Windows operating systems.

Dialog Boxes

Takes over your screen and allows you to "dialog" with the computer.

Directory (AKA Folder, sub-directory)

Allows you to organize files and other folders.

Disk Space

This is the place where your files live. The greater the disk space the more files you can keep. (See also Megabytes) More disk space is always better than less. You can never have much disk space.

Documents
Files you create and edit.

Document Files
Files we care about (memos, letters, pictures, etc.)

Double Click
To press the mouse button twice in rapid succession without moving the mouse between clicks.

Drag
To move an object on screen in which its complete movement is visible from starting location to destination.

Edit
To make a change to existing data.

File Cabinet
Metaphorically, the hard drive (and other kinds of storage media like floppy disks) which store files and folders.

Folder (AKA Directory, Sub-Directory)
Allows you to organize files and other folders.

  Folder Icons
  Collections of documents and other folders.

  Icons
  In a graphical user interface (GUI), a small, pictorial, on screen representation of an object, such as a document, program, folder or disk drive.

  Icon View

Allows you to see icons of folders and files primarily as icons with little information.

Keyboard
This if the primary text input device. It also contains certain standard function keys, such as the Escape key, tab, and arrow keys, shift and control keys, and sometimes other manufacturer-customized keys.

Kilo (K)
This is a unit of measure = 1,000. So 1,000 bytes is a KiloByte.

List View
Shows the icons but also orders the icons (often by name, but can sort the list in other ways) and shows more information about them.

Macintosh
The brand name of a family of personal computers (hardware) and an operating system (software) from Apple, introduced in 1984.

Megabytes (Mb)
Mega = million so Mb is 1,000,000 bytes. It's enough information for the computer to store one character (e.g. "h"), so 1mb text file = 1,000,000 keystrokes in that file. Just to confound the masses, although RAM and Disk Space do something completely different we measure both in megabytes. This leads to confusion.

MegaHertz (Mhz)
This stands for MegaHertz. A hertz is an electronics term. 1 hz = one cycle (or wavelength) per second. 1 megahertz = 1,000,000 cycles per second.

In computer jargon, Mhz measures how *fast* your CPU chip runs. Although it's more important to know the chip than the speed, if you're comparing the same kind of CPU chip then a higher / faster CPU speed (measured in MHz) is better than a slower speed.

Menu
Displays a list of commands, some with images next to them.

Modifier Keys
Keys that change the meaning of what you type.

Mouse
Pointing device that allows you to tell the computer what to do.

Operating System (OS)
System software that allows your computer to work.

Pointer (AKA Cursor)
The name of the arrow (or other shape) that tracks across the screen as you move the mouse (or other pointing device) around.

Random Access Memory (RAM)
This stands for Random Access Memory. You can think of this as the "space" where you computer does its processing. The more space you have the more processes you can run at the same time. More RAM is always better than less. You can never have much RAM.

Recycle Bin
Place where you put files and folders that you may later want to delete or get rid of. Compare Trash.

Resize Box

Allows you to change the size and shape of a window.

Right click

To press the right button on the mouse. (This is Windows specific. On a Mac running System 8 or higher, you hold down the Control key and then click to get the same effect.)

Save

Tell the computer to create a file on disk that has the information you've put into the document (usually typing).

Save As

Give the file a name and/or store the file in a certain place.

Scroll bar

Allows you to move around through your document.

Shut down

To quit all applications and turn off the computer.

Software

Instructions that tell the computer what to do.

System files

Allows our computer to work.

Trash

Place where you put files and folders that you want to delete or get rid of.

Volume Icons

Devices that hold files and folders.

Windows

1) The most widely used operating system for personal computers from Microsoft. (Software only. Other

companies manufacture the hardware that runs the Windows Operating System.) Compare Macintosh.

(Windows with a large "W".)

2) The thing you see on screen that contains a directory listing or the contents of a document. (Window with a small "w".)

CHAPTER 11
ONCE

Application Software. ___

Application Software is divided into six different groups: (1) Package Software,(2) Custom Software,(3) Shareware(Trial) Software,(4) Software Suite,(5) Freeware Software,(6) and Public Domain Software (7).

System Software as well as Application Software is installed by the User. Some System software and some Application software operate directly on the Computer Hardware, for example the Windows OS 8. The other Application Software that is dependant on the hardware, fall into the following categories:

Spreadsheet, Database, Graphics, Project Management, Multimedia, Medical, Scientific, Travel, Video and Audio, Education, and Multimedia Entertainment.

Rules in Computing. ___

The Rule of 30. ____

To prevent "Eye Fatigue" if you have to work on your Computer for long hours, look at something that is approximately 30 feet away for 30 seconds every 30 minutes.

The First Rule of Protection for Computers. __

The first Rule is **ACCESS** , if you give anyone access to your Computer, it means that you have given them your Key.

Do not give anyone access to your Computer

Once access is obtained, the Computer becomes vulnerable.

Access can be Physical Access or Software Access.

The second Rule is: **PRIVILEGE** Once privilege is obtained; the computer, is exposed to any malware and or damage to critical components and critical parts of the Computer registry, affecting the Operating System.

The third Rule is **RIGHTS** if rights is obtained, then The User Computer can be Destroyed, and any or all parts of the computer hardware and software is compromised, and the user computer is attacked by malicious software.

Note: Microsoft have created a " Malicious Software Removal Tool"

To get rid of this type of attack on User's Computers. This Tool is Free and available to download at http://www.microsoft.com

The fourth Rule is **PERMISSIONS** if an attacker get permission to access the User Computer, then he or she can Destroy or do anything they want to the user Computer and will have access to all the Security settings. The Computer is then considered lost and unrecoverable.

An example of the above Rule is:

A father talking to his son " JOHN".

John, here are **the keys** to the new Mercedes, Gold Edition

You can use the Radio and all the expensive electronics in the car and the built in Game system. You **do not have the right** to pick up any strangers or have any kind of alcohol beverages in the car.

You can drive around town, but you **do not have permission** to leave the State of New Mexico or to go more than 15 Miles in any direction.

Cleaning and Protecting the User Computer. ___

Software Utilities. ___

Software Utilities are small programs written to Clean the User Computer Registry and other parts of the Computer.

Some of these utilities are not Cleaners but work on other parts of the Computer Hardware and Software and are considered " Optimizers and or Tune Up Utilities.

The Registry is the most important part of the Computer, and keeping it clean and optimized will ensure that the user Computer will always be fast and productive.

The user computer hardware and software is always under attack by Viruses and Malicious Software, it is important therefore to keep the user computer clean and free from Viruses and or any attack that can harm the System.

The following is a list of Free Utilities designed to keep the Computer
Clean, and Secured. These utilities do not take the place of the
Application " Antivirus" which is a full Software program designed to "Protect" the user Computer from Viruses and have nothing to do with Cleaning or Tune-Up.

All user's Computers should have an Antivirus program, and one or more Registry Cleaner with a Malicious Removal Tool.

The Free Utilities are:

Glary Utilities version 5.175
Advanced System Care 10.4
Acebyte Utilities 3.0.2
Malawarebytes 2.0
Slim Cleaner
Windows Registry Cleaner
Windows utilities
Apache Open Office 4.0.0 Win_x86
AVG Free Antivirus_86_all_2021
LibreOffice_4.2.5_Win_x86
TuneUpUtilities 2021_en-US

Can be downloaded from the Internet. Go to **GOOGLE**, and type in the name of the utility, to download it.

CHAPTER 12
DOCE

The Fixed and Wireless Printer and Printer Standards.__

Many different kind of printers are available, but they all have something in common., the Print Engine inside the hardware., also all printers must meet the same international standards established by ISO and also Defacto Standards.

One of the most popular printer and also developer of the Printer print
Engine as well as many Defacto Standards is, HP or Hewlett Packard Company. The Standards developed by HP became very popular and was accepted as a "Defacto" standard, which means in simple terms a standard used and adopted, by everyone and available Free in some cases.

Printers developed by other companies local or international will use HP Print Engine as well as HP Defacto Standards. **HP developed many years ago de following standards now adopted worldwide.**

HPGL Hewlett Packard Graphic Language, PDL Postscript Description

Language, **HPGPIB** Hewlett Packard General Purpose Interface Bus, **PDF** Postscript Description File, etc.. These Standards are now used in every Printer.

In addition to the HP Print Engine, the other part of the Printer hardware that is very important is the Printer " Gamut".

The Printer Gamut is an Array of All possible Colors that can be printer and or Displayed. **The printer Gamut determines the Printer Resolution and capability to display and Print Millions of Colors following the International Color Standards.**

In the beginning we could only print and display limited colors, 4 to 8 colors only with the Standard; **RGB** Red, Green and Blue.

Later on, other color Standards were developed, such as: **CMYK**(0) or, **Cyan, Magenta, Yellow and K** <u>which represents zero (0) or (1). Pixel on/off.</u>

When the K bit or Pixel was turned on; the color was White, when it was off (0) the color was Black.

This Standard gave printers the capability to Print 64 Colors or more.

New Standards were developed, like **CROMALIN** from **Dupont, and PANTONE Certified Colors,** which allowed the display and printing of **Thousands and Millions of colors and shades.**

In the mean time, Computer Monitors were developed to use the same Standards to allow for the display of millions of colors to offer High Resolution for Graphics, Video and Multimedia displays.

These same standards are used on Television sets today to display HD High Definition Graphics, Sound and Video., and very **High Definition Displays (1080P) measured in Pixels.**

Printers must meet the Color Standards and should have a large GAMUT (64 Bit) or higher; to allow the Printer to Print High Resolution Text and Graphics in many colors.

The Printer Memory. _____

Most printers should have enough RAM Memory installed to store FONTS and other Graphic Software. Printers should have at least 4Gb of RAM Memory installed.

The Printer Ports. _____

Most Printers should have at least two (2) USB Ports. The Standard USB Port is USB 2.0, the New Standard for USB (Universal Serial Bus) is **USB 3.0 which is much faster.**

The USB Ports are used to connect the Printer to the Computer USB Port so that the User can Print to the

Printer., it requires a USB Cable that is included in most printers.

The Wireless Printer and Standard.

Most Printers today are built with Wireless capabilities, also called Wi-Fi. As with Computers, Wi-Fi is built into the computer hardware and contains an Adapter called a Wireless Network Adapter or Card.

This Wireless card is now built into every computer and Printer, to give the hardware wireless capabilities.

Wireless technology or Wi-Fi must meet the Wi-Fi Standard 802.11

That is defined as **802.11 a/b/g that originally only supported 54 Mbp and operated in 2.4 Mhz and 5.0 Mhz frequencies.**

802.11 a/b/g/n was developed later on, a new standard that increased the data rate to 100 Mbps and operated at higher frequencies.

The New Standard that was released last year is 802.11 a/b/g/n/ac and ad. This New Standard allows Wi-Fi to operate at very high Frequencies of 20 and 60 GHz. Increasing the data rate to Gigabit speeds and beyond.

Wi-Fi capable Printers are easy to use and setup, as no cables is required and the Printer is detected by the Network immediately as just another device. The built-in software will automatically setup the printer for the user.

Security Configuration and Analysis. _____

The security on a Computer running Windows 7 or 8 can be setup by using a SNAPIN called; Security Configuration and Analysis. This is one of the Snapins built in the MMC or Microsoft Management Console.

This Snapin will setup and configure the Security on the computer and will do an Analysis of the computer to verify that the security is configured correctly. A log file will be created that will allow the user to review the entire security setup on the computer. The log file can be short or very extensive with one or more than 20 pages, depending on the computer type and security requirements. The user can then print out these pages to review the security setup on the computer.

Setting up the Security on the Computer. __

Setting up the Security on the Computer is done is two parts:

Part 1: Creating the Security Configuration and Analysis, Snapin and the Security Database

Part 2: Creating the Security Template using the MMC Security Template Snap-in.

Create the Security Configuration and Analysis Snapin, and double click in the Console Root to open it.

When the Console Root is displayed, double click on the Security Configuration and Analysis item on the upper left of the console root to open it. First create the Database:

    To open an existing Database;

Right click the Security Configuration and Analysis scope item.
Click Open Database
Select a Database, then click open.
    Note: The Database will have the extension .sdb

        The database can be named anything, example: " security" but must always have the extension .sdb (security.sdb).

    To create a New Database:

Right Click the Security scope item
Click open Database
Type a New Database name, click open
Select a Security Template to import, then click open.

Creating a Custom Security Template using the MMC Snap-In called " Security Template".

Type MMC in the open box in the start button

From the file menu when the Snap In Console Root is displayed, choose" Add/ Remove Snap-In

In the Add/Remove Snap-In dialog box, choose Add

In the list of available Snap-Ins, Select " Security Templates" choose Add, choose Close, then choose OK.

In the MMC Main window, under the Console Root node, expand the Security Templates node, right click the root templates folder, and then choose New Template.

Type the Name and Description of the Template, example: Name: security

        Description: " Security Setup for Computers ", then   Choose OK.

This Saves your Template as an .inf file in the Windows\Security\Templates folder

In the Console tree, expand the Node for your new template, then browse to Local Policies, and then Double-Click Security Options, you will then see several settings you can customize.

After customizing the desired Security Settings, rightclick the root node for your new template, and then choose Save.

End

Automatic Configuration and Analysis.

After the Database is created, you may choose to have the
Security Configuration and Analysis Snap-In Analyze the
Computer automatically, by selecting:" Analyze my Computer Now", it will ask for the database, and when it is done analyzing, you can select" Configure my Computer Now", the Computer will be configured.

See list of Figures displayed below on the Security Configuration and Analysis process.

Security Template created.

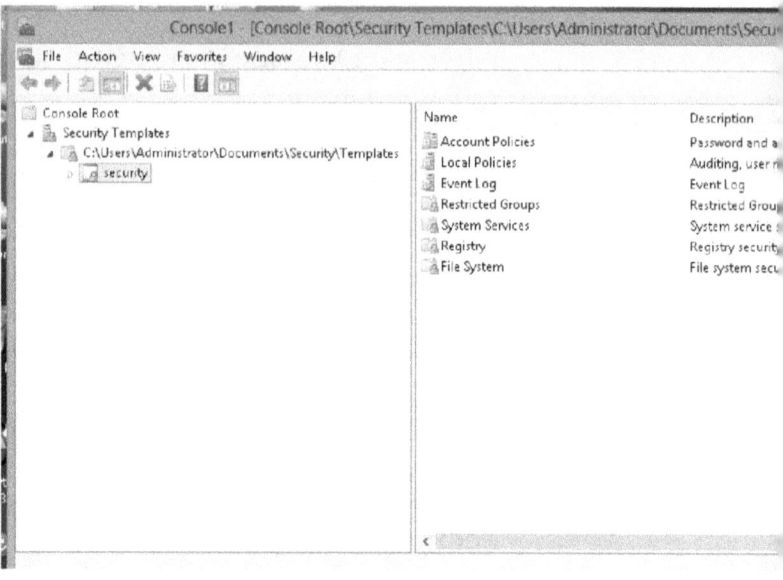

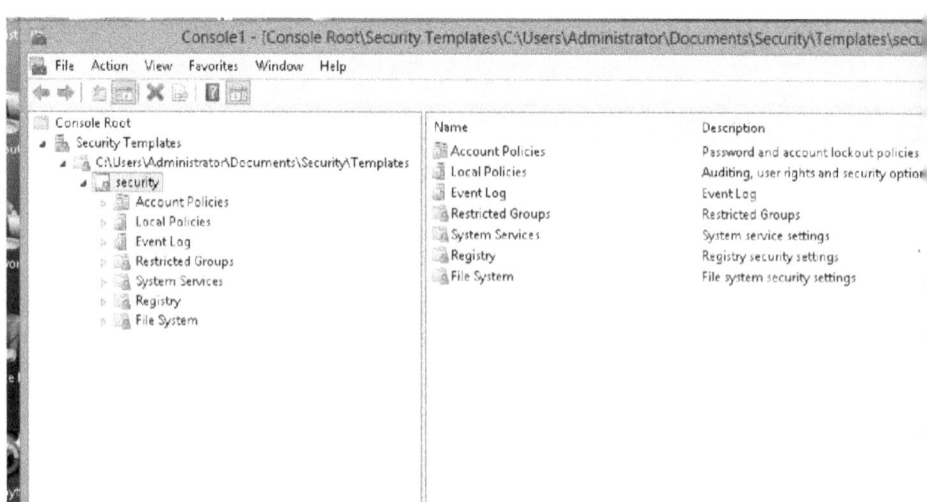

Security Template Expanded.

Security Options.

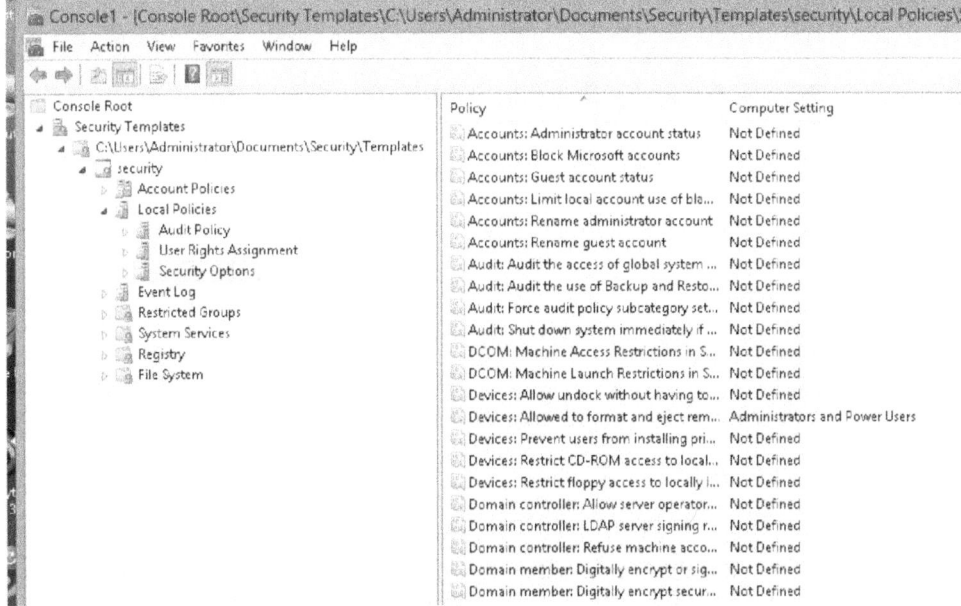

Local Policies expanded.

Using the Microsoft Management Console **MMC** and Creating Snap-Ins **is covered in detail and extensively in Chapter 7.**

A Word about Fonts and Word Processing Software.

A Font is a name assigned to a specific design of characters. Two basic types of Fonts are used in Word

Processing programs, Serif and SansSerif. A Serif Font

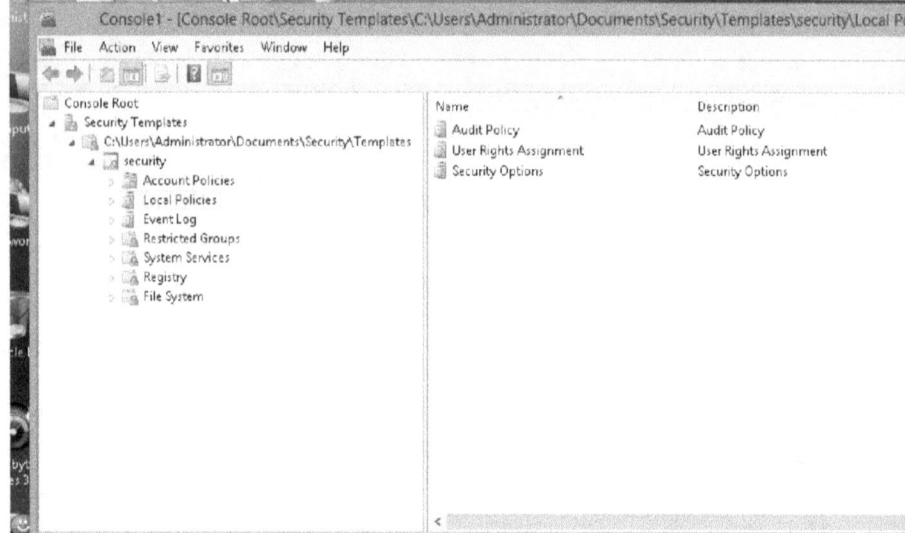

has short decorative lines at the upper and lower ends of the characters.

Sans means without. A Sans Serif Font does not have the short decorative lines at the upper and lower ends of the characters. **The Font Times New Roman; is an example of a Serif Font.** The Font Arial; is an example of a Sans Serif Font.

Font Size; indicates the size of the characters in a particular Font. Font
Size is measured by a measurement system called Points. A single Point is 1/72 of an Inch in height. **The Text you are reading in this book is a 14 Point with Titles in a 16 Point format.**

Each character is aprox. 5/36 (10/72) of an inch in height.

A Font Style; adds emphasis to a Font. Bold, Italic and Underline are examples of Font Styles.

Word Processing Software. __

Word Processing Software, is the most widely used type of Application Software. It is sometimes called a " Word Processor" , it allows users to create and manipulate documents containing Text and Graphics. One popular type of Graphic Image is Clip Art.

Clip Art; is a collection of Drawings, Diagrams, Maps and Photographs that you can insert into Documents. Word Processing
Software, usually includes public-domain clip art. Additional clip art and images are available in the public-domain on the Web.

Microsoft Office, which contains Word and other programs, is the most widely used Word Processor. They are other Word Processors available on the Web, such as **Open Office,** made by Apache, **a Free Word Processor in the Web area of Open Source.** This

Word Processor is available **Free to download at** http://www.openoffice.org

Additional Word Processing Features.

AutoCorrect; corrects common spelling errors

AutoFormat; automatically applies formatting to the text

Collaboration; include discussions and on line meetings

Columns; arrange text in two or more columns

Grammar Checker; proofreads documents for grammar, writing style, and errors.

Macros; a sequence of instructions the user records and saves to execute later.

Mail Merge; creates form letters, mailing labels and envelopes

Tables; organize information into rows and columns

Templates; a document that contains the formatting necessary for a specific document type.

Thesaurus; to lookup a synonym (word with the same meaning) for a word in a document.

Tracking Changes; for multiple users working on a document, to highlight or color-codes changes made by various users.

Voice Recognition; users can speak into the computer microphone and watch the spoken word display on the screen as they talk.

Web Page Development; allows users to create, edit, format and convert documents to display **on the World Wide Web (www.).**

Spread Sheet Software. ____

Is another widely used type of Application Software. Spreadsheet software allow users to organize data in rows and columns and perform calculations on the data, using built in formulas.

Charting .____

Another standard feature of spreadsheet software is charting, which depicts the data in graphical form. A visual representation of data through charts makes it easier for users to see at a glance the relationship among the numbers.

Database Software. ____

A database is a collection of data organized in a manner that allows access, retrieval and use of that data. The computer stores the data in an electronic format on a storage medium such as a hard disk.

Database Software is Application Software that allows users to create, access, and manage a database.

Presentation Graphics Software. ____

Is application software that allows users to create visual aids for presentations to communicate ideas, messages, and other information to a group. The presentation can be viewed as slides that display on a large monitor or on a Projection Screen.

Personal Information Managers (PIM). __

A personal information manager is application software that includes an Appointment Calendar, Address Book, Notepad, and other features to help users organize personal information.

Software Suite. __

Software Suite is a collection of individual programs sold as a single package. When installing the software suite, you install the entire collection of programs at once. Software Suites offer two major advantages: lower cost and ease of use.

Graphics and Multimedia Software. ____

This software includes computer aided design, desktop publishing, paint/image editing, video and audio editing, animation, multimedia authoring, and Web page authoring. This software is used by Engineers, Architect, Desktop Publishers and Graphic Artists.

Integrated Software. ____

Integrated software combines application software such as word processing, spreadsheet, and database into a single easy to use package. A widely used type of Integrated Software is Microsoft Works.

Personal Finance Software. __

Personal finance software is a simplified accounting program that helps home users and small office/home office users balance their checkbooks, pay bills, track personal income and expenses, track investments and evaluate financial plans.

Clip Art/ Image Gallery Application Software. __

This application software includes a clip art/image gallery which is a collection of clip art and photographs. The image gallery software may contain thousands of images. Many clip art image galleries provide fonts, animations, sounds, video clips, and audio clips.

A Word about New Technologies. ___

New Technologies that will change everything in 2014-2015 will be, 3D TV, HTML5, Video over Wi-Fi and super fast USB.

HTML5 is now the standard for writing Web pages (Hypertext Markup Language Version 5).

HTML5 will do away with the need for Audio, Video and interactive plug-ins. It will allow designers to create Websites that works the same on every browser, weather on a desktop, a laptop, or a mobile device. And it will give users a better, faster, richer Web experience.

- Instead of leaving each browser maker to rely on a combination of its inhouse technology and third-party plug-ins for multimedia.
- Website designers and Web App developers won't have to deal with multiple incompatible formats and workarounds in their efforts to create the same user experience in every browser.

Makers of operating systems and browsers such as Google chrome, Apple Safari, Opera, and Web Kit are all moving toward HTML5.

HTML5 is now completing its last march toward a final draft and official support by the World Wide Web Consortium.

USB 3.0 New Standard.__

USB 3.0 is now been used on modern desktop computers, replacing ports like Firewall, USB2.0, IEEE1394, DVI or Display Port except Ethernet. A computer may have several USB 3.0 ports delivering data to monitors, retrieving it from scanners, and exchanging it with hard drives.

USB3.0 can shoot full-speed data in both directions at the same time, an upgrade from USB 2.0 " half duplex" rates. USB 3.0 Jacks will accept 1.0 and 2.0 plug ends for backward compatibility, but USB3.0 cables will work only with 3.0 jacks. USB 3.0 is fast enough to allow uncompressed 1080p video (currently the highest-definition video format) at 60 frames per second.

<u>The new USB3.0 will also turn computers into real charging stations.</u>USB2.0 can produce 100 milliamperes (mA) of trickle charge

For each port, USB3.0 ups that quantity to 150 mA per device. USB2.0 tops out at 500mA for a Hub; the maximum for USB3.0 is 900mA.

The increased amperage of USB3.0 might let you do away with wall AC
Adapters of all kinds. Future desktop computers will have two internal Hubs, with several ports easily accessible in the front to act as a charging station. Laptop machines could multiply USB ports for better charging and access on the road.

The higher speed of USB3.0 will accelerate data transfers moving more than 20 GB of Data per minute. The format will be popular in mobile devices for consumer electronics as well.

The new USB 3.0 standard preserves backward compatibility by allowing older cables to plug into newer jacks, but newer cables like this one have extra pins that boost the data rate to 4.8 gbps.

That transfer rate will make USB3.0 five to ten times faster than other standard desktop peripheral standards.

Video Streaming over Wi-Fi . ___

Today's Wi-Fi will be left in the dust by the new Wi-Fi Standard 802.11 ac and 802.11 ad, both of which will be capable of carrying multiple video streams and operating at far higher data rates. These two new standards will be handling over-the-air data transmission at 1 gbps or faster., as a result users can have multiple high-definition video streams and gaming streams active across a house and within a room.

We look forward to using these new Technologies and the ones that are been developed in 2021 -2022

This is not the end.

www.ingramcontent.com/pod-product-compliance
Lightning Source LLC
Chambersburg PA
CBHW070233180526
45158CB00001BA/472